Home Sewn Quilts

Published by Sellers Publishing, Inc.

161 John Roberts Road, South Portland, Maine 04106
Visit our Web site: www.sellerspublishing.com
E-mail: rsp@rsvp.com

Edited by Robin Haywood
Translated from the Norwegian by Margaret Berge Hartge
Cover design by Ashley Halsey
Production layouts by Charlotte Cromwell

First published in 2015 as
Hjemme-Sydd by Trine Bakke
copyright 2015 © Cappelen Damm AS

ISBN 13: 978-1-4162-4585-8
Library of Congress Control Number: 2016931247

10 9 8 7 6 5 4 3 2 1

Printed and bound in China.

Home Sewn Quilts

31 Hand & Machine Stitched Projects for All Levels

Trine Bakke

SELLERS
PUBLISHING

CONTENTS

INTRODUCTION

I love to sew, and to make something that is beautiful and new from vintage fabrics. That said, it doesn't mean that I don't love to buy new fabrics! After all, I am part owner of a quilting business in the lovely town of Bærums Verk, about 40 miles outside of Oslo. The combination of new and old things makes me happy.

For me, sewing is the ultimate experience of enjoyment and meditation. The sound of a sewing machine is like a lullaby. To sit on the sofa and hand stitch is a lovely way to spend some time, and I'm able to daydream while my hands are doing something "useful."

I hope that this book will make you feel like pulling out all of your fabric scraps, and that it will help to increase the joy you feel when you are engaged in your hobby. If you are a beginner, or perhaps need a refresher, I urge you to take a look at Chapter 6 before you begin cutting. In that section I have included lots more information that I may not have had room for on the pattern pages. Be sure to check it out.

The quilting projects in this book are based upon simple shapes. However, even simple sewing projects become exciting when you use fun fabrics. Repurposing old clothes and flea market finds along with newly purchased fabrics allows you to set a personal stamp on anything you make. You can find an outlet for your creativity and at the same time make something useful.

If your favorite place is a good chair, you can sit there and do these projects by exchanging the sewing machine for hand stitching. This book will show you step-by-step hand stitching techniques, and you will, additionally, learn how to do contour embroidery, appliqués, and quilting. Everything you make does not have to be so perfect, because an appliqué can be very charming even if the stitches are a little messy.

The finished sizes of the projects in *Home Sewn Quilts* are approximate. Some of the projects feature vintage fabrics that have been laundered multiple times while others use straight-off-the-bolt wool or washed and felted wool. I've come to realize that it is difficult to provide you with precise measurements.

HAPPY STITCHING!
FROM QUILTING MISSIONARY, TRINE BAKKE

SOME TERMS I USE

The words quilt top (front side), backing (back side), outside, and inside (lining) will be used in the same way throughout this book.

The **quilt top** (front side) is the front, the most important part of a project. It is the piece that shows, and faces you.

The **backing** (back side) is still on the outside, but it is on the back of your project. The backing may not be as important as the quilt top when it comes to decorations.

The **inside** is, for example, the inside of a makeup bag. The inside can be seen when you open the bag, and in some cases, it is the lining.

NOTE

When noting fabric amounts, I use a 45-inch wide material.

The binding strip/bias tape is generally 2½-inches wide.

Part One:
Small Patchworks

CHAPTER 1

Begin: Play with Fabric

Make it simple: Gather pieces of different fabrics that will go well together. Decide whether you want to sew on a machine or by hand. Make your decision based upon what is the easiest for you. See Chapter 6 if you are looking for some help.

Easy-to-Make Linen Bag

FINISHED SIZE

About 13¾ x 23⅝ inches (35 cm x 60 cm) including handles

MATERIALS

- 1.6 yards (1.5 m) cotton belt webbing for two handle straps or 1.6 yards (1.5 m) x 6 inch (15 cm) wide fabric for sewing your own handles
- 17¾ inches (45 cm) fabric for the outside of the bag
- 17¾ inches (45 cm) lining fabric for the inside of the bag
- good-quality polyester thread

CUTTING

The seam allowance is ⅜ inch (1 cm), and front and back are exactly the same.

Cut two pieces of fabric, each to 14⅝ x 17 inches (37 cm x 43 cm) for the outside of the bag, and cut two pieces of lining fabric to the same size.

Cut the handles to a length between 23⅝ inches (60 cm) and 29½ inches (75 cm) long, depending upon the user's height and desired length. I am 5 feet 4½ inches (164 cm) tall and like handles that are 27 inches (69 cm) long.

This simple shopping bag has been sewn and lined so that no seams are visible. Even though that sounds like more work, it is remarkably easy to sew. Since the bag hasn't been quilted, it's possible to bunch it up into a small size and fit it into almost any purse.

DESIGN AND STITCHING | **TRINE BAKKE**

BEGIN

For each bag, start by cutting out the two pieces for the lining, two for the bag fabric, and two handle straps. Mark the center of the bag fabric, and measure a 4-inch (10 cm) space between the handle's two attachment points and mark. To make your own handles, cut out two pieces of fabric to your desired length. Make sure that the fabric is strong and not too rough. Fold the long outer edges toward the middle, then fold the length in two, press with an iron, and sew along the entire length. Either by hand or with your machine, sew with a polyester thread a few stitches at the handles' attachment points. Place the bag's lining and outside fabric on top of each other, right sides together, and sew them together at the bag's top edge. Repeat the process for the bag's second pair of fabrics, fold the seams flat, and press. Lay the front and back out flat, and place the pairs of fabrics on top of each other, right sides together, making sure that one lining piece is on top of the other, and that one bag exterior piece is on top of the other. Sew around all the edges, leaving an opening of 4 inches (10 cm) in the bag's lining for turning the bag inside out.

ASSEMBLE THE PIECES

To create a bottom for the bag, sew 2¾ inch (7 cm) long seams across the side seams at all four corners (both lining and bag fabric).

FINISH IN STYLE

Turn the bag inside out, press, and push the lining into the bag. Close the 4-inch (cm) opening in the lining with a few hand stitches.

Wool Scarf with Embroidery

This quick and easy winter scarf is made with a leftover row from the quilt on page 70. The assortment of wonderful wool comes from a manufacturer's sample kit of wool suiting, which provides a nice selection of patterns and tones. The pieces have been sewn together, then embroidered and paired with a neutral backing. This scarf is meant for looping several times around your neck, but feel free to shorten its length.

DESIGN AND STITCHING | **ANNE-KJERSTI JOHANSEN**

FINISHED SIZE
About 6⅝ x 86½ inches (17 cm x 220 cm)

MATERIALS
- 22 wool scrap pieces, about 7½ x 4¾ inches (19 cm x 12 cm) each
- fabric for the back side, about 7½ x 87¼ inches (19 cm x 222 cm)
- assorted colors of DMC Pearl cotton embroidery thread

OVERVIEW

Pieces of wool fabric that are approximately all the same size have been sewn together in a row. The row has 22 rectangular patches that are sewn then embroidered. Choose a fabric for the back side that is soft and pliable, such as linen or lightweight cotton. Place the row of patches on top of this fabric, right sides facing, *pin, and sew around all the edges, but leave an opening so you can turn the scarf inside out. Turn the scarf inside out, press, and stitch the opening shut.

*Sewing with wool

Wool fabrics are often looser and have a less stable weave than tightly woven cotton fabrics. It is a good idea when sewing with wool fabrics to place pins closely together, and to sew with a wider seam allowance than you would normally use.

BEGIN

Stitch the wool fabric pieces together in a row and press open the seam allowances. Each patch is then embroidered at the seam between the two rectangles. Many thread colors were used for the embroideries; DMC Pearl cotton thread works very well.

With right sides of the wool facing, place pins closely together and then sew the backing and scarf top together at the long edges. Press the seams and turn "the tube" inside out. Stitch the ends closed, and press.

"Four Patch" Wool Bolster

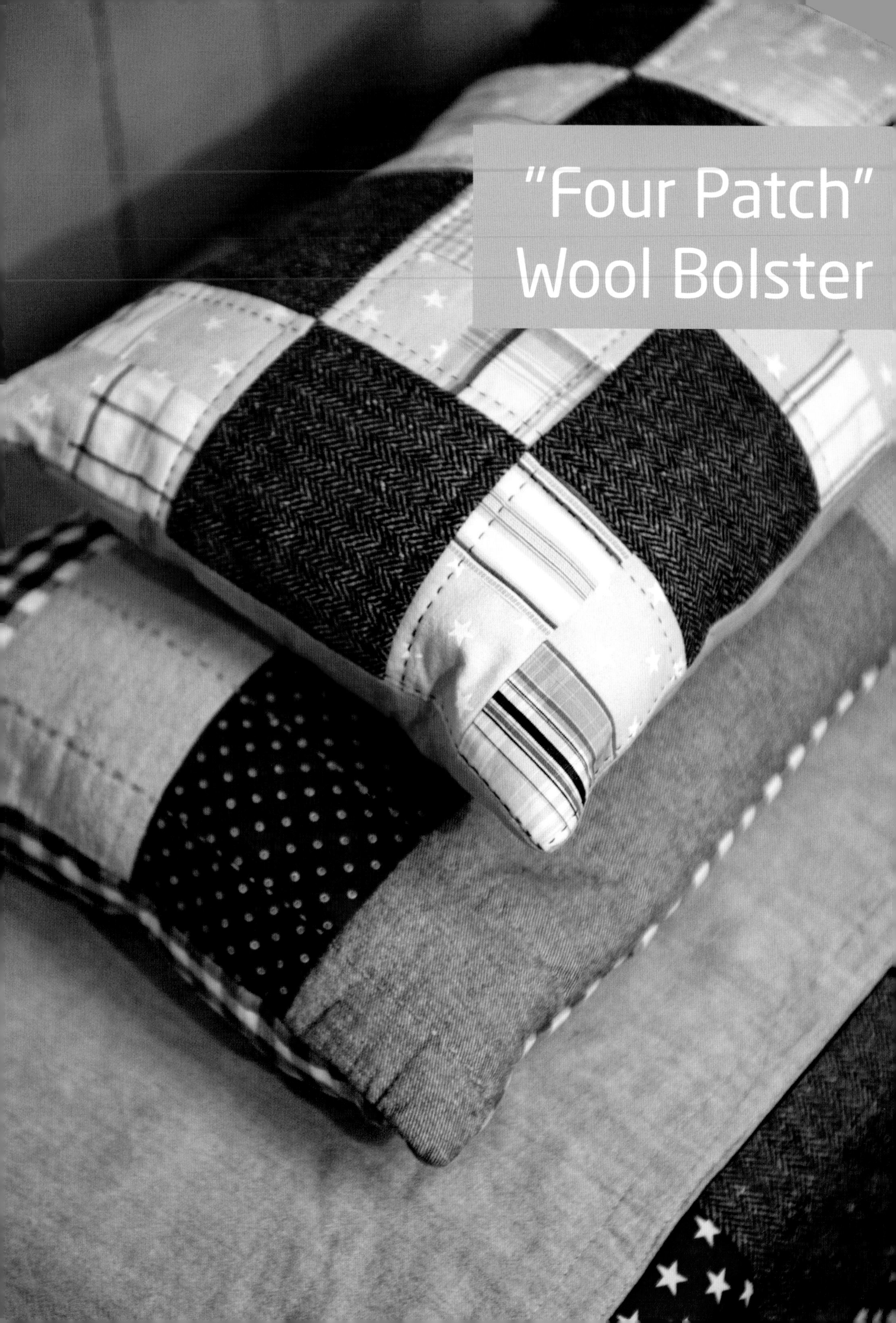

FINISHED SIZE
About 20 x 12 inches (50 cm x 30 cm)

MATERIALS
- seven large squares of brown wool fabric, each cut to 6 inches (15 cm)
- 16 small squares of light blue fabric, each cut to 4¾ inches (12 cm)
- 16 small squares of a different light blue fabric, each cut to 4¾ inches (12 cm)
- fabric for pillow back (I used the front of a shirt including the button placket), about 13¾ x 25½ inches (35 cm x 65 cm)

CUTTING
The seam allowance is ⅜ inch (1 cm).

The small squares are 2¾ x 2¾ inches (7 cm x 7 cm) (including seam allowance); the large ones are 4¾ x 4¾ inches (12 cm x 12 cm) (including seam allowance).

It is easiest to sew together patches that are from fabrics with the same thickness and quality. However, it is fun to mix different types of textiles. Some blocks on the front side of this pillow have been made with thin wool that has been used for garments – leftover fabrics from an Armani production, actually.

DESIGN AND STITCHING | **TRINE BAKKE**

OVERVIEW
The Four Patch blocks consist of two 4-inch (10 cm) wool squares and four cotton squares made from two different designs. Choose two cotton fabrics that are similar in tone. Next, cut out seven wool squares of the same size as the Four Patch blocks, and then sew one Four Patch cotton block onto a wool square, alternating blocks and squares to make the first row. Sew the second row together beginning with a wool fabric square. Begin the third row with a Four Patch block, and then sew all the rows together to make a quilt top. You may want to put batting or wool flannel under the quilt top, and sew a few stitches through the layers to quilt the pillow top.

FINISH IN STYLE
Place the quilt top and fabric for pillow back on top of each other, right sides together. Sew around all four sides and leave a space (about four inches) to turn the cover inside out, then hand stitch the opening shut.

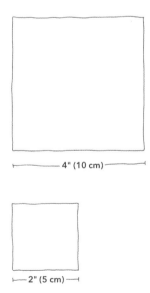

├───── 4" (10 cm) ─────┤

├─ 2" (5 cm) ─┤

See page 121 for pattern.

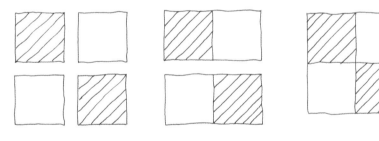

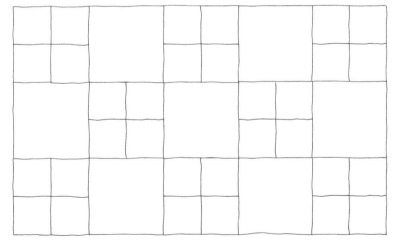

Christmas Stocking

FINISHED SIZE
About 21 x 10½ inches (53 cm x 27 cm)

MATERIALS
All in all, it takes six pieces of fabric to make one stocking.

- paper for tracing the pattern
- two muslin or other light-colored fabric pieces for the templates, each about 22 x 11½ inches (56 cm x 29 cm)
- two fabric pieces for the front and back, each about 22 x 11½ inches (56 cm x 29 cm)

  (If you plan to piece the finished front of your stocking like the photos, you'll need fabric scraps to cover this area, plus another solid piece of material for the finished back of the stocking.)

- two fabric pieces for the lining, each about 22 x 11½ inches (56 cm x 29 cm)
- 12-inch (30 cm) length of loop or cord

See page 120 for pattern.

I have Mirjam L. Beckhaug and Mias Landliv to thank for teaching me how to make Christmas stockings and for allowing me to put my own touch on this lovely project and share with you. We are fortunate, indeed.

DESIGN AND STITCHING | **TRINE BAKKE AND MIRJAM L. BECKHAUG**

BEGIN
Trace the stocking pattern (see page 120) on paper and cut out. Place the paper pattern on top of a double layer of muslin or similar fabric and cut out two templates. The muslin will serve as a template/base on which to build the pieced front and plain back of the stocking.

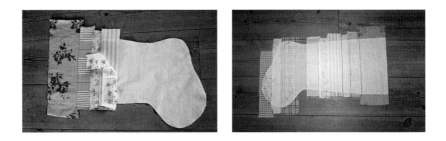

FRONT SIDE
Take the first muslin template and, using it as a base, lay out your pieced fabric design to create the front on top of it. Sew the design pieces together and press or, alternatively, use one length of fabric. Turn the front over so the muslin base is up, and facing you. Securely pin the front design to the base by placing straight pins, closely spaced, at a right angle to the seam, around the entire template. Stitch around the entire stocking template about ⅜ inch (1 cm)* from the edge of the template. Trim, cutting exactly around the muslin template's outline.

(*The seam allowance should be less than your regular seam allowance, so that you can leave this seam in place. For example, if you are usually using a ¼-inch [6 mm] seam allowance, this seam should be sewn ⅛ inch [3mm] or ³⁄₁₆ inch [5 mm] from the template's edge.)

If you want to quilt this stocking piece, do it now, and then set it aside.

LINING
Place the second muslin template on top of the folded fabric you'll use for the lining. Cut out the two lining pieces; one of the lining pieces will be mirrored to the front. Do not fasten the fabric template to the lining. Set the lining pieces and the other muslin template aside.

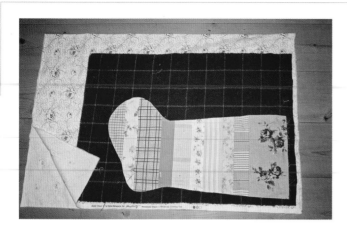

CREATE THE BACK SIDE

Using the second muslin template, make a mirrored finished back side of the stocking the same way as you made the front side. Stitch around the entire stocking template about ⅜ inch (1 cm)* (see note on previous page) from the edge of the template. Trim, cutting exactly around the muslin template's outline.

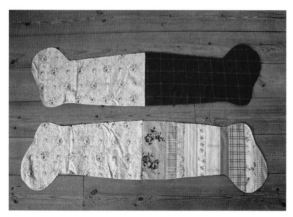

ASSEMBLE THE PIECES

Sew together the front pieced fabric design and one lining piece, right sides together, along the stocking's top edge where you normally insert your foot. Repeat the process for the stocking's finished back side. Press the seams.

FINISH IN STYLE

Place the two sewn stocking pieces over each other, right sides together. Pin all the pieces together and add a hanging loop (the loop is sewn into the side seam at the top, on the heel side). Sew around all the edges with a regular seam allowance, *but* be sure to leave an opening in a lining seam so that you can turn the stocking inside out. I usually choose a spot on the leg toward the heel for this opening. With your scissors, make small nips around the rounded edges (heel, toes) of the curves so they lie flat. Turn the stocking inside out, press, and push the lining back into the stocking. With a few hand stitches, sew the opening in the seam shut.

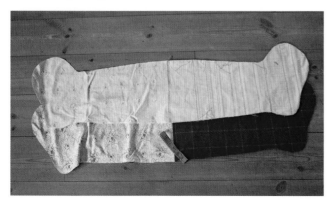

Cross-body Passport Bag

FINISHED SIZE
About 7½ x 9 inches (19 cm x 23 cm)

MATERIALS
- vintage linen tablecloths and fabric from favorite dresses and shirts
- lengths of straps and cords from bags that you no longer use
- 6-inch (15 cm) zipper
- a sturdy strap (such as cotton belt webbing), about 46 inches (117 cm) long for the strap
- button (optional)

CUTTING
All measurements include a ⅜-inch (1 cm) seam allowance.

Back side
Cut one piece of fabric for below the zipper (bottom): 8⅝ x 14¼ inches (22 cm x 36 cm), folded in half with right sides facing out, so that it measures 8⅝ x 7⅛ inches (22 cm x 18 cm).

Cut another piece of fabric for above the zipper (top): 8⅝ x 5¼ inches (22 cm x 13 cm), folded in half with right sides facing out, so that it measures 8⅝ x 2⅝ inches (22 cm x 6.5 cm).

Cut one piece of fabric for the inside of the zippered pocket: 8⅝ x 10 inches (22 cm x 25 cm).

Front side
Cut one piece of fabric for the front side (#1): 8⅝ x 10 inches (22 cm x 25 cm).

Cut another piece of fabric for the outside pocket on the front side (#2): 8⅝ x 7½ inches (22 cm x 19 cm) (I stitched a small hem across the top of piece #2 as it becomes a front outside pocket).

Cut one piece of fabric for a pocket on the front (#3): 8⅝ x 6¼ inches (22 cm x 16 cm), folded in half with right sides facing out, so that it measures 8⅝ x 3⅛ inches (22 cm x 8 cm).

Lining
Cut two pieces of fabric to line the inside of the bag: 8⅝ x 10 inches (22 cm x 25 cm) each.

Cut one piece of fabric for a pocket lining: 8⅝ x 6¾ inches (22 cm x 17 cm).

This bag will keep your travel essentials handy: your passport, boarding pass, eyeglasses, phone, and other travel essentials will all be within easy reach. If you'd like a bit more security, you can easily wear the bag under your jacket because it's not too bulky. There are a couple of places where you'll have to hand stitch, but for the most part, this bag comes together pretty quickly on your machine.

A good lightweight linen would be a great choice for the bag, but keep in mind that it's not an easy fabric to work with, nor is it as stable as cotton, so place pins closely together and baste seams here and there when working with this material.

DESIGN AND STITCHING | **TRINE BAKKE**

OVERVIEW
Making the bag may seem complicated because it has multiple pockets and details, but the sewing instructions are, briefly, as follows: First you sew the front of the bag, then the back, followed by adding a lining to a pocket on the back side and two on the front, then, finally, adding the inside lining. You finish each part of the bag first, and then you sew the parts together following the instructions given for sewing the Easy-to-Make Linen Bag on page 12.

BEGIN
Sew fabric tabs to each end of the zipper; see illustration below.

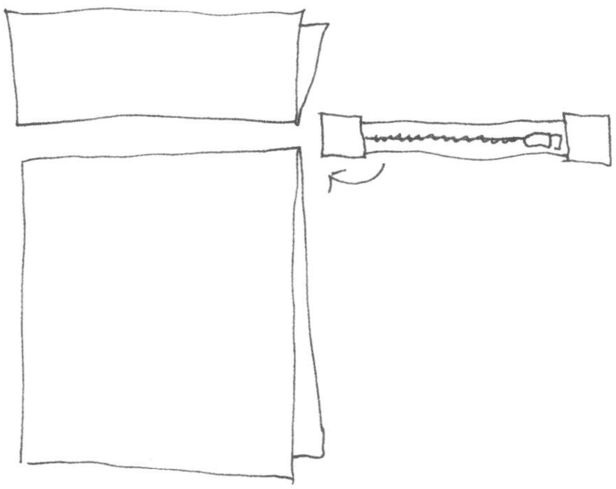

BACK SIDE
Place the zipper on a table, right side up, then pin the folded bottom piece to the zipper's fabric tabs, one on each side. Repeat with the folded top piece. Sew the fabrics in place with a sewing machine equipped with a zipper foot. This sewn piece with a zipper is the bag's back side. See illustration.

Place the piece of fabric for the inside of the zippered pocket behind the assembled back side. Place the right side facing in and the wrong side facing out. Pin the pieces together, and sew a basting stitch around all four sides ⅜ inch (1 cm) from the fabric edge.This seam is only for holding the pieces in place.

FRONT SIDE

Place the largest piece of fabric (#1) on the table with the right side up. Place the pocket piece (#2) of fabric on top with the right side up. Both of the fabric pieces align at the bottom, and the fabric's hem lies toward the top of the bag. The hem will be the pocket's top. Next, place the small pocket fabric (#3) on top of the already assembled fabric pieces, again aligning the bottoms. Stitch around the sides of the pockets and along the bottom, using the ⅜-inch (1 cm) seam allowance – the stitching is to hold all the parts in place. You will sew another seam later.

Sew vertical seams to create pockets that are sized for the items that you want to carry in your bag. I always need my sewing glasses and a pen, and have made small pockets that will accommodate these things. A pocket with enough space to fit a boarding pass is also a good idea.

LINING

Make the bag's front and back lining exactly the same size as the bag's outside front and back sides. Cut an additional piece of lining, fold it in two, and make a pocket for one of the bag's lining sides. Use the same method to make this pocket as you used for the bag's front pockets.

STRAPS

For the bag's shoulder strap, use a length of cord you already have on hand or sew one from a piece of fabric. To make one, cut out a piece of fabric measuring about 46 x 3 inches (117 cm x 8 cm). Make sure that the fabric is strong and not too rough. Fold the raw, long outer edges toward the middle, then fold the length in two, press with an iron, and sew along the entire length.

A STRAP FOR CLOSURE

Cut a length of fabric about 8 x 2½ inches (20 cm x 6.5 cm) and sew with right sides together; the finished width should be about 1 inch (2.5 cm). Turn it inside out and press. Make a buttonhole at one end or add a cording loop using, for example, a piece from an old

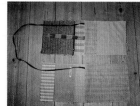

hoodie cord. Attach the cord loop to the strap's bottom seam, where you later will fasten the loop to a button. I always cut off straps and pocket openings from old garments before I discard them. That way, I always have these useful fabric parts on hand for different projects.

ASSEMBLE THE PIECES

Pin one end of the shoulder strap to the front, and indent about ½ inch (1.5 cm) toward the center. Repeat with the other end and pin to the back, with the ½-inch indent toward the center back. The two front and back pieces, now connected by the shoulder strap, must always be carried together when you move from the sewing machine to the ironing board.

Place the non-loop end of the closure strap about 1½ inches (3.8 cm) from the left side (as you look at the inside back) and stitch.

Tips

This passport bag is a perfect purse companion to carry inside a larger bag, so that your most valuable items do not get misplaced. It can be a "guest" inside many purses. You can change the bags you carry frequently – from a shopping bag, to a purse, to a briefcase – without having to repack your essentials each time. Just grab the passport bag with your valuables from one bag, and place it in the next without repacking anything – so smart!

Place one piece of lining with right sides together on top of the piece of fabric for the bag's front outside, and pin them together. Sew the pieces together at the bag's top edge, sew a zigzag seam along the raw edges, and press. Place the other piece of lining on the bag's outside back and repeat.

Open the front and the back so they lie flat on top of each other with right sides together, and make sure that the lining fabrics are on top of each other and that the bag's outside fabrics are on top of each other. Check that all the parts of the closure strap and shoulder strap are placed away from the seams that you will sew. Pin all the pieces together around the edges, but leave a 4-inch (10 cm) opening in a lining seam. You will use this opening to turn your bag inside out. Sew around all the

edges with a rounded seam at the bottom of the front and back and trim excess fabric.

Turn the bag inside out, press, and push the lining inside the bag, sew the opening in the lining shut with some hand stitches, and press along the bag's upper edge. Sew a button in place on the bag's front side; its location depends on where you attached the loop strap and how long it is.

CHAPTER 2

Next: Cut, Appliqué, and Sew

In this chapter, I'll cover the basics of cutting, sewing, and appliqué, either by hand stitching or machine sewing.

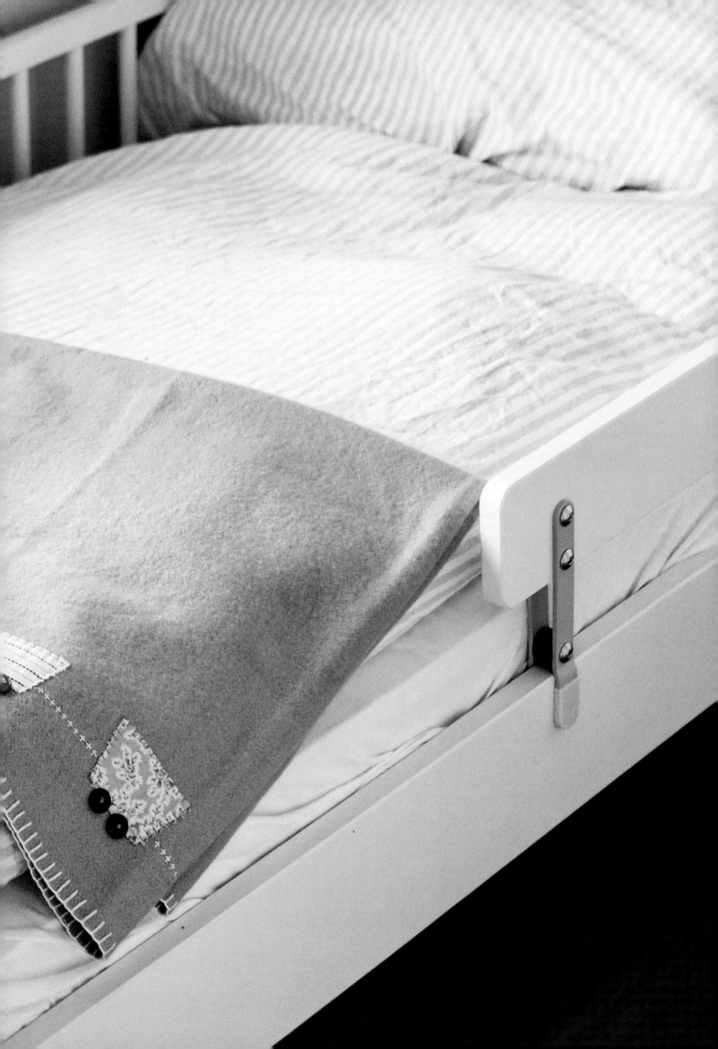

Linen Runner with Appliquéd Hexagons

FINISHED SIZE
About 48½ x 22½ inches (123 cm x 57 cm)

MATERIALS
- 1½-inch (3.8 cm) ready-made templates or templates made by cutting 1½-inch (3.8 cm) hexagons from pattern paper
- one piece of linen fabric for table runner, 48½ x 22½ inches (123 cm x 57 cm)
- eight fabric scraps for the hexagons, 4 x 4 inches (10 cm x 10 cm) each
- cotton Pearl embroidery thread (I used a light gray color that matched the linen fabric's color, so that the stitching would not show up too much on the reverse side of the runner.)
- bias tape for raw edges, if your piece of linen does not have hems or selvage edges on all sides.

1½ " (3.8cm)

See page 121 for pattern.

This is a very satisfying project that you can finish in one evening. I've made it with linen and have stitched appliqués at each end and finished it with bias tapes along the raw edges. Simply, appliqué hexagons on a piece of linen, sew, and you are done – so simple and super fast!

DESIGN AND STITCHING | **TRINE BAKKE**

BEGIN
Decide where on the table runner you want to place the hexagon appliqués. I placed mine in such a way that the runner looks proportionally good in relationship to my dining room table. Use the full-size pattern on page 121 (Indigo Pillow with Hexagons), trace it to your pattern paper, and then trace it to your fabric. Once they are cut with the seam allowance, press, baste the hexagons in place, and then sew them onto the linen piece using embroidery stitches (see page 111 for information on stitching).

Press hexagons with the seam allowances basted in place. See the next project on page 30 (Indigo Pillow with Hexagons).

FINISH IN STYLE
Sew bias tape along all of the linen fabric's raw edges. My linen piece only had raw edges at the short ends. Fold the bias tape nicely under at the beginning and at the end of the covered edges. See page 115 for help with bias tape or binding strips.

Yes, I love hexagons, so here is another project that uses them! The hexagons have been arranged in a row at the bottom of the denim fabric. You can choose, according to your mood, whichever method you want to use to appliqué the hexagons onto the fabrics. You may even want to just embroider the hexagons' outline on the pillow.

DESIGN AND STITCHING | **SARA BOLSTER WITH RIE NORUM AND TRINE BAKKE**

BEGIN
You can either buy ready-to-use 1½ inches (3.8 cm) hexagon templates, or you can make your own templates by tracing the template on page 31. The correct length for each of the hexagon's sides is 1½ inches (3.8 cm).

FINISH THE HEXAGONS AND APPLIQUÉ
Place a hexagon template on a fabric's wrong side. Pin it in place with one or two straight pins. Cut out the hexagon with seam allowances around the whole shape.

Be very careful to make even seam allowances. This is very important for the finished result. Place the cut piece of fabric with the template pinned in place on an ironing board with the template facing you. Fold the seam allowance over the template on one of the hexagon's sides, and iron it to hold it in place. Fold and iron one side after the other until you have folded in and ironed all of the hexagon's seam allowances. Finish by pressing the whole

Indigo Pillow with Hexagons

FINISHED SIZE
About 19¾ x 19¾ inches (50 cm x 50 cm)

MATERIALS
- one piece of denim fabric, 29½ x 43¼ inches (75 cm x 110 cm)
- four different pieces of fabric for the hexagons, 4 x 4 inches (10 cm x 10 cm) each
- bias tape for the larger back side fabric, 21⅝ inches (55 cm) long
- fabric for two button loops, 6 x 11¾ inches (15 cm x 30 cm) each
- 1½-inch (3.8 cm) ready-made templates or templates made by cutting 1½-inch (3.8 cm) hexagons from pattern paper
- two buttons
- bias tape or binding strip, 20½ inches (52 cm) long

CUTTING
Cut the front side to 20½ x 20½ inches (52 cm x 52 cm).
Cut the smallest back side to 20½ x 10 inches (52 cm x 25 cm).
Cut the largest back side to 20½ x 18½ inches (52 cm x 47 cm).
Cut the two loops to 2 x 4¾ inches (5 cm x 12 cm) each.

hexagon. Carefully remove the pin and the cardboard template. Steam press the hexagon both on the front side and the back side. Your hexagon is now ready to be appliquéd onto a fabric. You may choose small, invisible stitches for sewing on the appliqué, or use large, rough stitches that are decorative just by themselves.

POSITION THE HEXAGONS
Appliqué the hexagons onto the front pillow cover's top or at the bottom. For our pillow cover, we spaced the first three hexagons evenly apart, and then placed the last hexagon, in the same row, farther apart from the others.

ASSEMBLE THE PIECES
Sew a hem along one long side of the small piece of fabric for the pillow cover's back side. Fold another piece of fabric, and make loops (see page 32 "Brick Wall" Bolster). Attach the loops to one of the large piece of fabric's long sides. This piece of fabric is the second one to make up the pillow cover's back side. The loops should be fastened lying downward. Attach bias tape to the same long side to cover the whole length, also where the loops are attached. Then fold the loops upward and fasten them with cross stitches.

Place the back side's two fabric pieces on top of each other and overlap, so that they together are of the same size as the pillow's front side. The small fabric piece with the hem should be under the larger piece with the bias tape. Sew buttons on the smallest piece of fabric. Match up the buttons' locations with the location of the loops, and choose a colorful thread for sewing, so that the thread colors become a decoration in addition to the closure mechanism.

Button the two back pieces together.

FINISH IN STYLE
Place the entire back side and the front side on top of each other, right sides facing. Sew around all the pillow's edges. Sew a zigzag seam over all the raw edges and trim the seam allowances at the corners. Turn the pillow cover inside out through the opening in the back of the pillow.

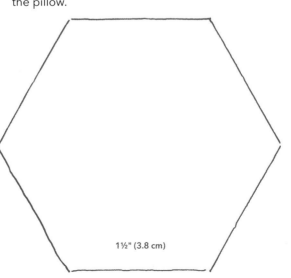

1½" (3.8 cm)

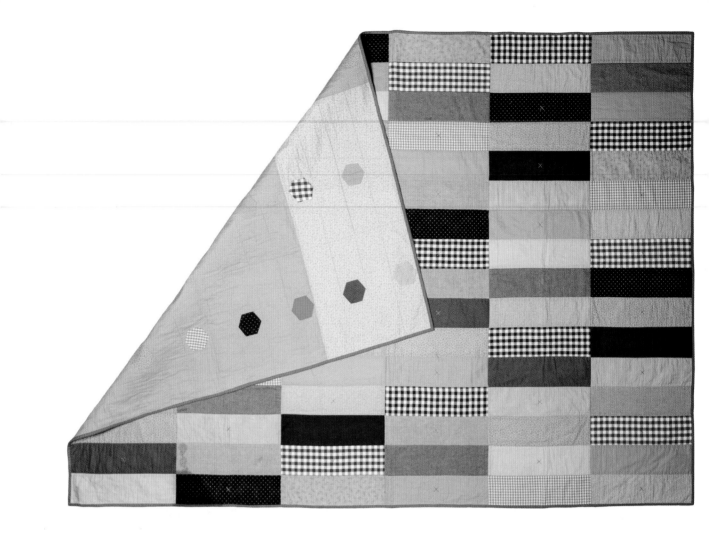

"Brick Wall" Bolster with Appliqué

(see matching quilt on page 66)

FINISHED SIZE
About 26¾ x 14⅛ inches (68 cm x 36 cm)

MATERIALS
- eight fabric pieces for the pillow's front side, 15¾ x 6 inches (40 cm x 15 cm) each
- one piece of fabric for the back side, 15¾ x 47¼ inches (40 cm x 120 cm)
- one piece of fabric for the loops, 4 x 6 inches (10 cm x 15 cm) (optional)
- buttons (optional)
- DMC Pearl embroidery thread for hand quilting
- **pillow insert:** You may want to repurpose an old down comforter and make your own insert, or sew an insert case and fill it with polyester stuffing. Make the insert the same size as the pillow cover, 26¾ x 14⅛ inches (68 cm x 36 cm).

CUTTING
The seam allowance is ⅜ inch (1 cm). Cut eight rectangles to 14⅛ x 4¼ inches (36 cm x 11 cm) each.

Make a long pillow cover from leftover fabric logs . . .

DESIGN AND STITCHING | TRINE BAKKE AND RIE NORUM

BEGIN
If you didn't make the quilt that matches this bolster, then you may be able to make this from scraps that you have on hand. If you did make the quilt, you can make and/or use eight of the leftover fabric logs to make the front of a pillow cover. First sew the log pieces together into rows, and then sew all the rows together. There are two logs, placed horizontally, in each row.

ASSEMBLE THE PIECES
Place your quilt top on top of a piece of flannel or batting, and quilt vertical seams across the top 2 inches (5 cm) apart. Notice that we were not shy about choosing a quilting thread that contrasts with the log fabric colors.

BACK SIDE
Measure the pillow cover's front side, and make a back in the same size. Our pillow's back cover has buttons with loops and overlapping parts. See the overlap drawing on page 113.

The back side's smallest part has been hemmed along one edge.

The back side's two parts overlap so that the back side ends up the same size as the pillow's front side.

FINISH IN STYLE
Place the finished back side and front side on top of each other, right sides together. Pin the pieces, and then sew around all the edges. If not using a buttoned back, then leave a 4-inch (10 cm) opening for turning before sewing closed. Use a good-quality, strong thread for these seams. The insertion of a pillow insert requires durable seams. Sew a tight zigzag seam over all the raw edges; you won't have to worry if the pillow is used roughly and requires multiple launderings.

Choo-choo Baby Blanket

FINISHED SIZE
About 50½ x 33½ inches (128 cm x 85 cm)

MATERIALS
- wool blanket hemmed with white blanket stitches
- matching thread for appliqués
- contrasting colored thread for the embroidery between the train cars
- 56 buttons for wheels (if each train car has two buttons; I used 53)
- three fabric scraps for the train engines, 5 x 3½ inches (13 cm x 9 cm)
- 25 fabric scraps for the train cars, 2½ x 3½ inches (6 cm x 9 cm) each

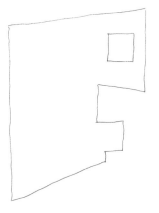

See page 124 for pattern.

All the cute babies we know would love to have their own soft wool blanket with fun train appliqués along the edges. I have used an already-hemmed, light blue wool blanket for this project. However, you may choose to cut out a blanket of the right size from a larger one, and then hem it by hand sewing blanket stitches around the edges. Or you may make a quilt with one solid background fabric, appliqués, batting, backing, quilting, and bind-off edging.

It is easy to care for this blanket. I use a wool setting on my washing machine for washing, and then place the washed blanket to dry, overnight, on top of a terrycloth towel flat on the floor.

DESIGN AND STITCHING | **TRINE BAKKE**

PREPARATION
I washed the wool blanket in the washing machine, on a wool setting, before I started to sew on the appliqués. I also have washed, before use, all the fabrics that I will be using for the appliqués so there will be no unhappy shrinkage surprises after the blanket's first laundering.

APPLIQUÉS
You can appliqué the train and train cars by hand stitching or sewing on a sewing machine. Trace the patterns onto a fusible interfacing. (Trace each pattern separately on the paper side.) Trim and iron the interfacing pattern pieces onto the back side of the fabrics you are going to use for the appliqués using an iron with a low heat setting. Cut the appliqué pieces out precisely following the shape's outline, and remove the paper.

When you have completed cutting out all the different pieces with the interfacing on the back side of the fabric, spread them out on a table. The two corner train designs contain eight cars (excluding the engine), and the train design that extends along the long edge of the blanket contains nine cars (see photo on next page). Leave a space between each train when you pin them on the blanket. They should all go in the same direction. I promise you that this placement will make a harmonious-looking blanket.

Tip

Do you need a refresher on how to sew blanket stitches? See page 112.

Iron all the appliqués onto the fabric using a low heat setting.

Sew blanket stitches around all the appliqué shapes using a thread color that matches the appliqué's color, and sew by machine or hand. Decide before you start which thread color you are going to use for the blanket stitch, taking into consideration that this thread will show on the back side of your blanket. I used a thread color that is pretty similar to the blanket's color for the stitching, and for sewing on the buttons.

ASSEMBLE THE PIECES

Sew on the buttons as train car wheels. Three of the train cars have only one big button. All the others have two buttons. I chose from my button jar, both white and colored buttons, and I chose to alternate the colors on the train cars. This is a golden opportunity to use treasured button collections. Generally, I have used similar buttons on each train car, but this is not always true. It is easy to run out of them when such a large number is required. I deliberately used button colors that complement my fabric selections and matched them up on the different train cars. When you use the blanket, make sure to often check that the buttons are securely fastened to avoid any choking hazard.

FINISH IN STYLE

Use tailor's chalk to mark the location of the chain connection between the train cars. It will look best if the connections are placed a little below the train cars' center line. Use a chain stitch to embroider the chain connection between the train cars. I discovered that a white thread looks the best. At first, I tried to embroider with a blue thread that matched the blanket in color, but that just made the train look as if the train cars were not connected.

Linen and Wool Bag with Dresden Appliqué

FINISHED SIZE

About 19 inches wide x 17¼ inches high (48 cm wide x 44 cm high) without handles

MATERIALS

- 16-inch (40 cm) zipper
- 12 fabric scraps for the appliqué flower on the front of the bag, 4 x 4 inches (10 cm x 10 cm) each
- one fabric scrap for the flower's center, finished size about 6 inches (15 cm) diameter
- two fabric tab pieces for the zipper, about 4 x 8 inches (10 cm x 20 cm)
- fabric for the bag's outside, about 21⅝ inches (55 cm); I used three different fabrics at 6 inches, 15⅝ inches, and 21⅝ inches (15 cm, 40 cm, and 55 cm)
- fabric for the bag's inside 21⅝ inches (55 cm)
- 100% natural cotton batting (one package for a crib-size blanket is usually enough for two bags)
- fabric for the zippered pocket, 21⅝ inches (55 cm)
- tracing paper for a 10-inch (25 cm) Dresden template
- 1.6 yards (1.5 m) cotton belt webbing for handles. The webbing will be enough for two handles with a maximum length of 29½ inches (75 cm) each. Adjust the length of the handles to fit your height. My handles are 27½ inches (70 cm) long, finished length. I am 5 feet 4½ inches (164 cm) tall.

CUTTING

Overall seam allowance is ⅜ inch (1 cm), unless otherwise noted.

Cut two pieces for the upper back side, 19¾ x 4⅜ inches (50 cm x 11 cm) each.

Cut two pieces for the lower back side, 19¾ x 15 inches (50 cm x 38 cm) each.

Cut one piece of batting for the front side, 21⅝ x 19¾ inches (55 cm x 50 cm).

Cut one piece of batting for the upper back side, 21⅝ x 6 inches (55 cm x 15 cm).

Cut one piece of batting for the lower back side, 21⅝ x 15¾ inches (55 cm x 40 cm).

Trim the batting after you have quilted all the pieces for the bag.

See page 127 for pattern.

The gray-brown linen, wool, and flannel fabrics that are used in this bag provide the perfect backdrop for the Dresden block flower to take center stage. It elevates it from the everyday workhorse it is to an heirloom piece that you'll cherish.

DESIGN AND STITCHING | **TRINE BAKKE**

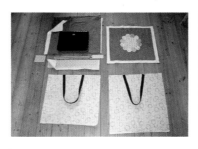

BEGIN

The bag has been sewn using the same pattern as the Cross-body Passport Bag shown on page 22 and the Easy-to-Make Linen Bag shown on page 12. The back side's upper part has a pocket with a zipper closure.

APPLIQUÉ

Refer to the detailed information on appliqué and hand stitching at the back of the book (see pages 111-112). Begin by making a template of the flower using tracing paper (see the complete pattern on page 127), piecing it together and then employing invisible stitches to appliqué the flower on the bag's front side. Once you finish, cut open the fabric behind the flower appliqué to remove the tracing paper templates. Place the bag's front fabric piece on batting and quilt.

Sew the back side's two upper fabric pieces together along one of the long sides, press, and fold the two sides over each other, right sides out. Place batting between the two layers and quilt. Repeat the process for the back side's lower piece. Sew fabric end pieces onto the zipper. Finish off the bag's back side by sewing the zipper in place between the upper and the lower parts. Use a zipper foot when sewing.

Place a single piece of fabric under the bag's back side. This fabric will be the pocket's inside, and must be placed with the right side facing the wrong side of the bag's back side.

ASSEMBLE THE PIECES

Lay out all the pieces as explained on page 13, Easy-to-Make Linen Bag, and sew them together. Sew a false bottom seam at each corner at the bottom of the bag. These seams should each be 2⅜ inches (6 cm) long. See Cross-body Passport Bag, page 22, for more information.

FINISH IN STYLE

Sew a seam around the opening at the top of the bag, about ¾ inch (2 cm) below the top edge.

This generously sized yet practical bag could quickly become your go-to carrier for laundry, bed linens, and more. With a wide elastic band at the top, it's easy to carry wherever you are going, whether you're traveling back and forth from a vacation home, your child's room, or from your third floor down to the laundry room in the basement.

DESIGN AND STITCHING | **TRINE BAKKE**

Wool Bag with a Ten-point Star Appliqué

OVERVIEW
The star is appliquéd to the front of the bag in the center position.

BEGIN
Use ready-made plastic diamond templates or make your own by tracing the diamond pattern on page 126. Be sure to cut out all the pieces precisely by following the cutting lines. Machine or hand stitch the diamonds together and press. I've discovered that it's a good idea to appliqué a circle over the center of the finished star, if your star's center becomes as imprecise as mine. Hand stitch between the 10 paper-pieced fabric that's covering the templates and be certain that the star's points are intact. Next, attach the star to the bag's front wool fabric by sewing along its outer edges using invisible hand appliqué stitches. You will have to use your needle to work the star's points into place while you are sewing. Trim the star points' seam allowances down to as narrow a width as you dare, and push them under the surface so that the points become as even as possible. The paper templates will help to keep the shapes intact. This technique is called "needle turn appliqué" because you

FINISHED SIZE
About 20 x 32 inches (51 cm x 81 cm) including handles

MATERIALS
- plastic templates: 3-inch (8 cm), 30-degree diamonds and possibly circles from Paper Pieces (www.paperpieces.com) or your local quilt shop
- 43⅜ inches (110 cm) cotton belt webbing for handles
- wool fabric for the outside, 25¾ inches (65 cm)
- fabric for the lining, 25¾ inches (65 cm)
- flannel fabric for the batting, 25¾ inches (65 cm)
- 10 fabric scraps for the star, 8 x 4 inches (20 cm x 10 cm) each
- one piece fabric scrap for the circle at the center of the star, 3¼ inches (8 cm) in diameter
- 1⅛-inch (3 cm)-wide elastic band, 27½ inches (70 cm) long
- cord for carabiner

CUTTING
All the bag's pieces have been cut the same size: 23¼ (59 cm) high x 21⅝ inches (55 cm) wide. Start by cutting out two pieces of the same size in the wool fabric. One piece will be the bag's front side and have the appliquéd star, and the other piece will be the bag's back side. Then cut two pieces of lining in the same size as the bag's front and back sides. Next cut out, in the same size, the two pieces of old flannel. The flannel will be used as batting between the bag's outer fabric pieces and the lining. Cut two handles that are 21⅝ inches (55 cm) long.

turn the seam allowance under the appliquéd shape using your needle. Look on YouTube for videos that demonstrate this technique.

When you have attached the star to the bag's front wool fabric, cut an opening in the wool fabric at the back of the star. Use this opening to remove all the paper templates. The templates are only meant to help you sew the shapes, and should not be left in place. Cut carefully, because it is easy to cut through into the star's fabric. I cut around the star's outer outline leaving only a narrow, even seam allowance. You can also trim the stars' seam allowances at the same time.

ASSEMBLE THE PIECES
Place the bag's front fabric piece on top of a layer of flannel, and sew in the ditch around the whole star. Then, baste the wool fabric and the flannel fabric together around the outer edges to hold them in place.

Sew the rest of the pieces together as explained on page 13, Easy-to-Make Linen Bag. The bag's handles, which are sewn in place along with the bag's top stitching, are centered in the middle of the bag, and the distance of the space between the bag and the top of a handle is 4½ inches (11.5 cm). The bottom of the bag, with its rounded edges, has a 3-inch (8 cm) "fake bottom" seam in each corner.

Fasten a cord with a carabiner on it to the inside of the bag, so that you can attach keys or a small coin purse. Place the cord inside the lining's side seam when you sew the sides together. As you sew the bag together with right sides facing, you will leave an opening in the lining for turning the bag right side out, and one opening in a lining seam about 1¼ inches (3 cm) from the top of the bag. This opening is for inserting the elastic band that you will add later. Make sure to fasten your thread well at the beginning and end of your seams, at the openings.

FINISH IN STYLE
Next, you'll make a casing for the elastic band. As explained above, you will need an opening to insert an elastic band. If you did not remember to make this opening, just cut up a lining seam exactly where you want the elastic band to end up. You must remember to fasten the seam well at each side of the hole. Sew two parallel seams around the whole bag through all the layers. The space between the seams will become the casing for the elastic band. Sew the top seam about 1¼ inches (3 cm) below the bag's top edge, and the next seam 1⅜ inches (3.5 cm) below this seam. Pull a wide elastic band through the casing using a large safety pin. Pull on the elastic band until you have the desired amount of gathering or opening, and sew the elastic band's ends together. If you wish you can sew the opening in the seam shut.

See page 126 for patterns.

Sailor's Ship Wheel Runner

FINISHED SIZE
About 59 x 19⅝ inches (150 cm x 50 cm) laundered

MATERIALS
- six different pieces of cotton fabric for the blocks, 10 x 10 inches (25 cm x 25 cm) each
- six wool fabric scraps, 10 x 10 inches (25 cm x 25 cm) each (I used scraps from wool blazers I get at flea markets.)
- fabric with an open, large pattern for the border, about 51¼ inches (130 cm). If you want to use several fabrics to make the borders, you will only need about 23⅝ to 27½ inches (60 cm to 70 cm).
- backing and cotton batting, about 67 x 27½ inches (170 cm x 70 cm)
- 12-inch (30 cm) of 45-inch wide fabric for binding strip
- cotton Pearl thread
- a needle with a large eye and a sharp point
- small appliqué pins, about ⅜ inch (1 cm) long

CUTTING
The seam allowance is ⅜ inch (1 cm) and is included.

Cut six squares for the appliqués, each measuring 8⅝ x 8⅝ inches (22 cm x 22 cm).

Cut the borders on the runner's long sides 6¼ inches (16 cm) wide.

Cut the borders on the runner's short sides are each 5¾ inches (14.5 cm) wide.

See page 118 for pattern.

DESIGN AND STITCHING | TRINE BAKKE

BEGIN
I've used an unexpected fabric for this project: washed and felted wool for the appliqué pattern, which is then sewn to a cotton block, with a wide cotton border. The pattern can be found on page 118, so begin by tracing the templates for the appliqués on your choice of paper, and cut out the shapes. Pin the paper templates with straight pins to the wool. Cut along the paper templates to get the complete sailing ship wheel shape in wool. Choose cotton fabrics for the appliqués' background fabrics that are in contrast to the wool fabrics you used for the wheels.

Place the wool sailing ship wheels on top of the cotton fabric squares, and pin them in place with tiny appliqué pins. My appliqué pins are about ⅜ inch (1 cm) long. It is a good idea to use these pins, because your sewing thread will not get caught up in these needles while you are sewing. I chose a cotton Pearl thread and used large stitches for these appliqués. I chose a thread color that is in contrast to the fabric colors I selected.

I stitched these appliqués over a period of time, and I did not refer back to a previous wheel block while I was working on another. The blocks are witnesses to this fact. If you study the picture of the runner, you will see that the appliqués are deliciously unlike when it comes to the placements on the blocks, and the distances between the wheel shapes vary. Some of the shapes are sharp and meet each other, while others swim loosely around on the block. This was not an intended design, but it turned out to be a beautiful imprecision. In the same vein, the stitches go this way and that way. I am constantly surprised by how imprecise my work is. Just the same, I think that I create beautiful things. The joy of sewing is more important to me than a measuring tape.

ASSEMBLE THE PIECES
Sew borders onto the row of appliqué blocks. The quilting is done on a sewing machine, and you sew in the ditch at all the seams. In addition, sew around the contours of the sailing ship wheels and around the squares in the middle. The borders have been quilted everywhere with closely spaced, parallel seams.

The 2¼-inch (6 cm)-wide border has been cut out from a piece of fabric, pieced as necessary to get one that is long enough, ironed double with the right side facing out and sewn to the runner's right side. Afterward it was folded over to the runner's back side, and hand stitched in place with a hem.

FINISH IN STYLE
I was a little nervous about washing this runner. The wool had been laundered, but the wool sailing ship wheels were rather loosely appliquéd due to my sewing technique, so there was a real danger that the pieces could disappear when laundered. If you want to avoid this problem, you must appliqué the pieces with tightly spaced stitches and felt the wool before you cut out the shapes. My own solution to this problem is to pat the pieces back into their places and let them dry flat.

CHAPTER 3

Quilt: Patchworks

Patchworks are wonderful projects that are the perfect gateway to making bed-size quilts. In this chapter, you'll find "mini" quilt designs for table runners, a zippered button bag, a tissue pack holder, and a handy quilted sleeve to keep a pair of scissors and a small pincushion.

Blue Denim "Four Square" Table Runner

FINISHED SIZE
About 24⅜ x 11⅜ inches (62 cm x 29 cm) finished and laundered

MATERIALS
- six denim fabric scraps from various lightweight blue jeans, 4 x 8 inches (10 cm x 20 cm) each
- six pieces of fabric for the Four Squares blocks, 4 x 8 inches (10 cm x 20 cm) each
- one piece of shirt front or other fabric for the backing, 13¾ x 25⅝ inches (35 cm x 65 cm)
- cotton batting, 13¾ x 25⅝ inches (35 cm x 65 cm)

CUTTING
The seam allowance is ⅜ inch (1 cm).

Cut 24 square fabric pieces, 4 x 4 inches (10 cm x 10 cm) each.

Cut two 4¾ inch (12 cm) wide squares of the same fabric for the borders

Sew the whole quilt top together before cutting out the shirt front for the backing.

Finished square fabric pieces: 3½ x 3½ inches (9 cm x 9 cm) each

Finished borders: 4½ inches (11 cm) wide

I've mixed up this quilt top using different fabric squares of the same size. Every other square has been cut out of blue denim fabric, and the quilt top has been sewn together using an old shirt front with a button placket as backing. This is a very simple way of finishing a table runner. You sew the quilt top and the backing together, right sides facing, just as you would join the front and the back of a pillowcase. Instead of adding a pillow insert, you could just press the quilt top and the backing flat together, and use it as a table runner. I have added batting to give some extra "plush." By using the button placket to turn your project right side out, you do not have to worry about a binding strip, or sewing shut the opening that would otherwise have been used for turning the project inside out.

DESIGN AND STITCHING | TRINE BAKKE

OVERVIEW
Make six Four Square blocks, and sew them together to make a quilt top with 2 x 3 blocks, or 4 x 6 square fabric pieces. Then measure the length of the short sides and cut an equally long border piece for each side, 4¾ inches (12 cm) wide.

FINISH IN STYLE
Place the quilt on top of batting, right sides together, pin or baste, and quilt both pieces together. Trim the quilt's edges. Cut a piece of fabric from an old shirt front the same size as the quilt.

Place the quilt and the shirt front backing on top of each other, right sides facing, and sew around the whole runner (see photo). Trim the corner seam allowances. Sew a zigzag seam along all the seam allowance edges, turn the runner inside out, and press with an iron. You may want to sew a seam around the entire runner, on the right side at the edges, to keep the layers in place.

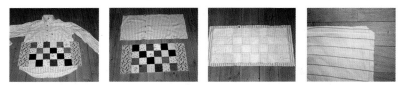

Red "Brick Wall" Runner

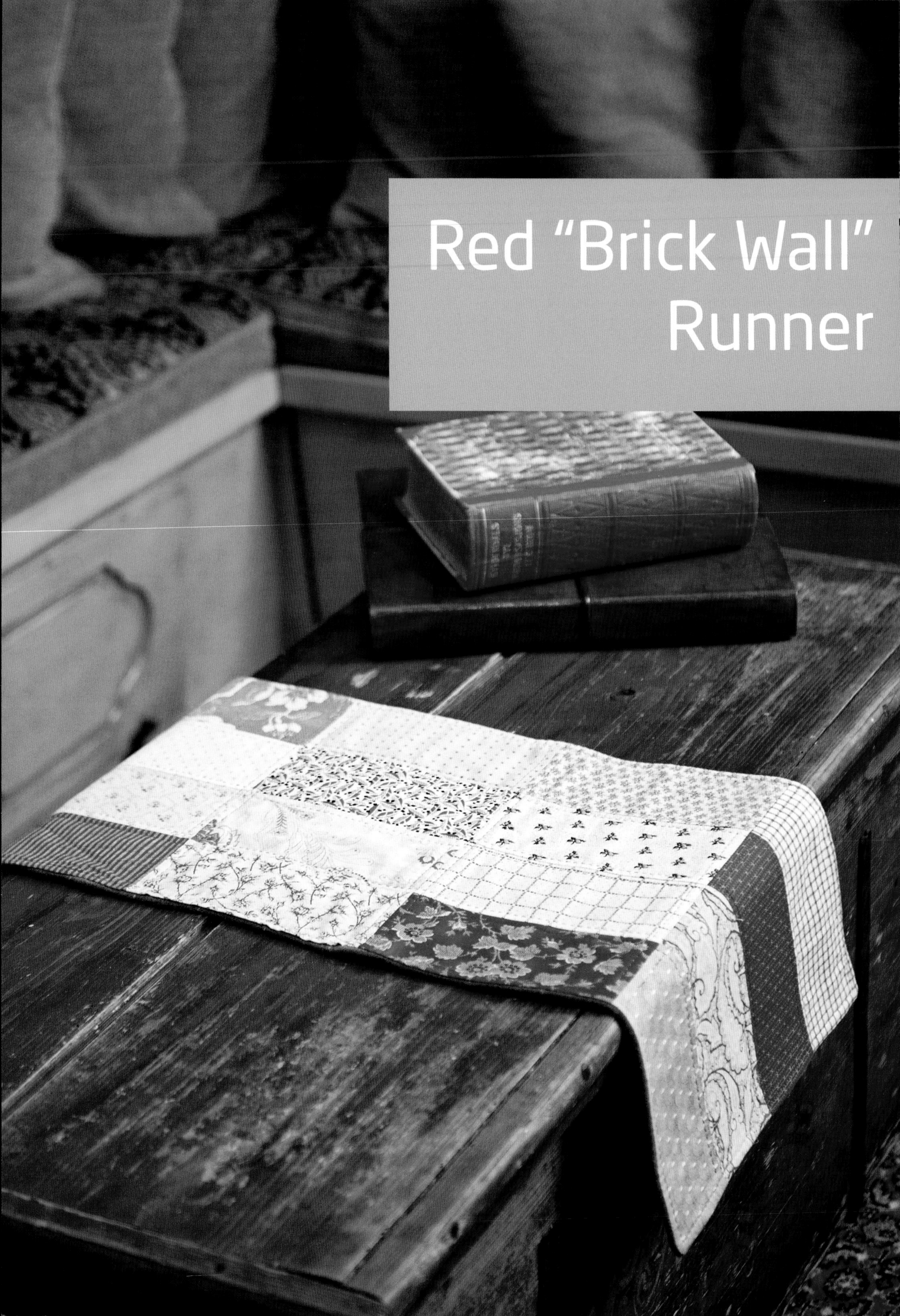

FINISHED SIZE
About 13⅜ x 30 inches (34 cm x 76 cm)

MATERIALS
- a washed, and slightly felted, piece of a wool blanket for the batting and backing 15¾ x 31½ inches (40 cm x 80 cm)
- 16 fabric pieces for the top, 6 x 10 inches (15 cm x 25 cm) each

CUTTING
The seam allowance is ⅜" (1 cm).
Cut 16 exactly 8¼ x 4⅛ inches (21 cm x 10.5 cm) each.

This small table runner was very simple to make. I used a piece of an old wool blanket that I felted, slightly, for both the batting and the backing. The small table runner was inspired by Miele Brinck, who gave me a bag filled with vintage fabric scraps from France.

DESIGN AND STITCHING | **TRINE BAKKE**

OVERVIEW
First, you'll sew the fabric pieces together to make a row, then sew the four rows of rectangles together to make the quilt top.

ASSEMBLE THE PIECES
Place the quilt on top of a wool blanket fabric, right sides together. Pin it in place, and sew around all the edges, leaving an opening for turning the quilt right side out. Trim the seam allowances at the corners, turn, and press with an iron. Stitch the opening shut.

FINISH IN STYLE
Sew around the whole quilt, including across both the short and long sides, to hold the pieces in place. You may want to do this stitching by hand, because not all sewing machines are able to sew through the layers without shifting the layers and making everything crooked. Regardless, it is a good idea to baste the pieces together before you start quilting. It is also a good idea to use a walking foot on your sewing machine, and to sew with a long stitch setting. Pinning all the layers together before you baste also helps.

Go to page 113 to read more about finishing.

Coffee or Tea?

FINISHED SIZE:
About 9¾ x 6¾ inches (25 cm x 17 cm)

MATERIALS
- the front of an old shirt including the button placket, or a piece of fabric measuring about 11¾ x 8 inches (30 cm x 20 cm)
- six fabric pieces, 3½ x 3½ inches (9 cm x 9 cm) each
- one piece of batting, 11¾ x 8 inches (30 cm x 20 cm)
- 10-inch (25 cm) piece of fabric or cord for a hanging loop

If you add a hanging loop onto your quilted cup mats while you are sewing the sides together, you can use them as hot pads. See the attached hanging loop in the photo below, right.

This "mug mat" is very straightforward and is the perfect entrée for those who are just beginning to get comfortable with quilting. There cannot be a simpler project! The mat can be used to protect your tabletop or as a pot holder.

DESIGN AND STITCHING | **TRINE BAKKE**

BEGIN
Sew the six squares together.

ASSEMBLE THE PIECES
Place the assembled quilt top on top of batting and quilt (see page 107), then trim all the edges. If you would rather avoid quilting, you may want to choose synthetic iron-on batting for this project.

FINISH IN STYLE
I used a piece of fabric from a shirt front for the backing. Place the quilt and shirt front on top of each other, right sides facing, and sew around all the edges. Turn the mat right side out through the shirt's button placket, button shut, and press. If necessary, sew a few stitches to hold the layers in place. See drawing on page 113 to leave an opening for turning the bag inside out.

FABRIC PIECES WITH DIFFERENT DIMENSIONS?
Use the same techniques, but cut larger fabric pieces. Cut all the fabric pieces 4½ inches (11 cm) wide, and sew them together in rows. Make one row using only one piece of fabric, and the other row with several squares sewn together.

TO WASH OR NOT TO WASH?
Cotton batting that is sandwiched between the quilt top and the backing will give the mat a nice, soft, wavy texture after the first washing. It is best to dry your quilted mat only for a short while in the dryer, and then finish drying it flat. Slightly pull on the cup mat edges while it is damp to adjust the shape so that it lies flat. You may want to lightly press it with an iron when it is completely dry.

Zippered Button Purse

FINISHED SIZE
The size depends on the length of your zipper. The bag shown here is about 4½ x 4 inches (11 cm x 10 cm).

MATERIALS
- a zipper with a 4-inch (10 cm) chain length (you may need to adjust for length)
- fabric for two purse linings and two purse outsides, each about 8 inches (20 cm) in length. (If you're going to use the adjusted size for Courthouse Steps block, then you need a length of about 12 inches [30 cm].)
- two pieces of thin batting, 6 x 6 inches (15 cm x 15 cm) each
- four buttons and a little embroidery floss for stitching

Adjusting the zipper length
The following are general cutting instructions regardless of the size of your zipper, and assume that the zipper has a tape that is a little wider than ¼-inch (6 mm) on each side of the chain.

Measure the zipper's chain length and add ½ inch (1.5 cm) to this measurement. This is the required width for all the fabric pieces. You can choose any length you want. Cut out two pieces of fabric for the purse's outside following your own dimensions. Cut two pieces of lining fabric of the same size, adding ½ inch (1.5 cm) to the height dimension. This extra height will be the nice, visible lining edging that will be concealed when the zipper is closed.

(Note: These instructions work when you do not have a pieced purse front, but are using just one piece of fabric. If you use a pieced block for the purse's front, you must trim it to the right size after it has been quilted.)

In this project, you'll be installing a zipper at the top of this cute "button purse." Use any zipper you have on hand, and cut to the length mentioned here or adjust the size if you'd like it larger.

DESIGN AND STITCHING | **ANNE-KERSTI JOHANSEN**

BEGIN
Sew a variation of the Log Cabin block (see diagram on page 57), or use just one piece of fabric for the purse's front. Place the fabric over a piece of batting, and fasten the two layers together by sewing a few seams. Repeat the process for the purse's back side. Since I live in Norway, I used Rasterquick, which may not be available everywhere. I suggest a Quilt Fuse layout grid, which features a 2-inch (5 cm) grid, so you may have to adjust the overall size of the button purse. The sewn, center fabric square measures ¾ x ¾ inch (2 cm x 2 cm), so if you increase the center square size on the 2-inch (5 cm) grid and use a ¼-inch (6 mm) seam allowance, the remaining pieces would be proportionately larger.

+ ½" (1.5 cm)

x 2

Opening

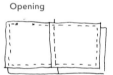

The zipper is attached at the transition between the lining fabrics and the outer fabrics.

ASSEMBLE THE PIECES
Place the purse's front side and the lining fabric on top of each other, right sides facing. Sew them together at the top edge. Press the seam toward the lining fabric. Repeat the process for the purse's back side and lining. Sew the purse's sides together in this way: Place the two sewn purse pieces on top of each other, right sides facing, making sure that the front of the purse is over the back of the purse, and that the corresponding lining fabrics are on top of each other. Pin in place, and sew around all the edges, but leave an opening for turning the purse inside out. Make sure that the opening is located on the lining fabric.

Fasten your thread well at the beginning and at the end of the seam where the opening is located. Trim the corner seam allowances, turn the purse inside out, and press. There should be a ¼-inch (6 mm)-wide strip of lining fabric that is showing at the top of the purse on the outside. Stitch the opening, where you turned the purse inside out, nicely shut either by hand or machine.

FINISH IN STYLE
Hand stitch the zipper to the purse's outside by sewing a combination of small, decorative stitches and invisible stitches. The zipper should be attached right at the transition between the purse's lining fabrics and front and back fabrics. The zipper's chain starts and ends exactly at the purse's side seams. Fasten the seam well, and reinforce the zipper at the outer edges.

The zipper's ends are sewn together with two buttons at each end. Sew through all the layers: one button, two layers of zipper tape, and one more button. Use embroidery floss, and repeat the process at the zipper's other end.

Quilted Tissue Holder

FINISHED SIZE
5⅛ x 3½ inches (13 cm x 9 cm)

MATERIALS
- two pieces fabric and lining approximately 7 x 7 inches (18 cm) for the lining and the outside fabric
- a six-inch (15 cm) length of batting
- 2¾ inch (7 cm) fabric for the binding strip or 12 inches (30 cm) of bias tape

CUTTING
Cut two pieces of the outside fabric and two pieces for the lining, 6 x 6¾ inches (15 cm x 17 cm)

Cut one piece of batting 6 x 6¾ inches (15 cm x 17 cm).

Cut two binding strips 2 x 6 inches (5 cm x 15 cm) each.

You may think that making a tissue pack holder is something of an extravagance, but trust me, on those days when you have a sniffle, it will bring you nothing but pleasure and delight.

DESIGN AND STITCHING | **TRINE BAKKE**

OVERVIEW
Sandwich together a lining fabric, batting, and an outside fabric. The lining fabric is placed with the right side down, and the outside fabric with the right side up. Baste the sandwich together and quilt; you could also use a fusible batting between the layers if you want to avoid basting.

ASSEMBLE THE PIECES
Fold the binding or bias tape in two along its length with right sides out, and iron. Sew it in place at the quilted piece's two short sides, on the lining fabric's side. Place the binding or bias tape and the quilted piece's raw edges on top of each other, and sew a seam with a ¼-inch (6 mm) seam allowance. Iron and fold the bias tapes toward the outside fabric. Sew the binding or bias tape in place on the outside by sewing along the edges.

FINISH IN STYLE
Fold the tissue holder together with the inside out, and sew the seams at the tissue holder's top and bottom. Sew a zigzag seam at the raw edges. Turn the holder inside out.

OTHER VARIATIONS
You can make a tissue holder much quicker by omitting the batting and lining the inside. If you choose to make one this way, use a heavier fabric, for example, a denim or a tweed. The sewing process is the same for all holders.

You may also wish to make holders for different purposes following your own measurements. A holder for wet wipes is a perfect gift for new mothers, or you can make a holder for table napkins, panty liners, or other feminine products.

This fun pincushion and scissors bag are both small yet practical items that will work very well for transporting your sewing implements. The pincushion has been made to be rather flat, so that you can easily put it into the scissors bag next to your scissors.

DESIGN AND STITCHING | **TRINE BAKKE**

"Log Cabin" Pincushion and Scissors Bag

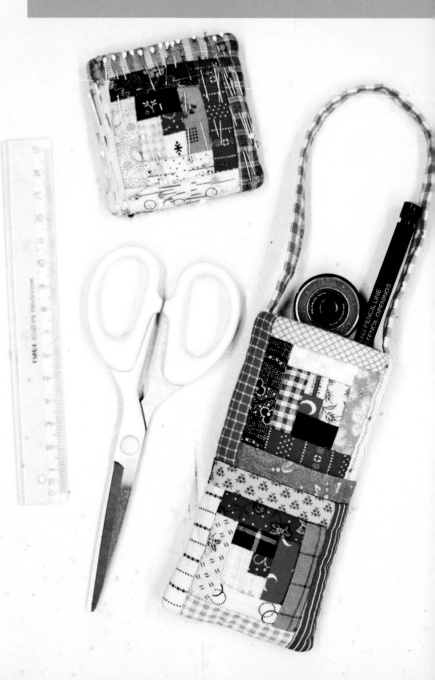

OVERVIEW

For this project, you'll be photocopying the pattern to paper and creating a template to use for sewing it to your fabric with your sewing machine. There are five miniature Log Cabin blocks – a finished block is a 3-inch (8 cm) square. I have used grid paper and plain copy machine paper to make multiple copies of the Log Cabin template; vellum paper is also a good choice.

All the fabrics that I have used for these projects have come from my fabric scraps box. I started collecting fabric scraps and filling up the box many years ago. Presently, it contains mostly leftovers from previous projects and odd-shaped scraps that have been cut into 1-inch (2.5 cm) wide strips.

SEWING THE PAPER TEMPLATES

Place the fabric on top of the paper's back side and sew, following the stitching line, on the front of the paper template. Choose a tight stitch-length setting on the sewing machine to help perforate the paper – this makes it easier to tear the paper away when the blocks are sewn together at the end.

For this Log Cabin block, start with a red piece of fabric, with the right side up, and place it in the X position on the template. Next, place a lightly colored

FINISHED SIZE

scissors bag: 2¾ x 5½ inches (7 cm x 14 cm) without strap; the strap measures about 5 inches (13 cm) sewn in place

pincushion: 2¼ x 2¼ inches (6 cm x 6 cm)

MATERIALS

- one length of fabric for the strap, 11 inches (28 cm) (I used a piece of an old apron string.)
- fabric scraps, 1 inch (2.5 cm) wide
- one piece of thin batting for the pincushion, 3 x 3 inches (8 cm x 8 cm)
- two pieces of thin batting for the Log Cabin square and the lining, 6 x 6 inches (15 cm x 15 cm) each (I used Quilters Dream Supreme batting for the pincushion and Soft Touch for the scissors bag.)
- one piece of fabric for the pincushion's back side, 3 x 3 inches (8 cm x 8 cm)
- one piece of fabric for the bag's lining, 6 x 6 inches (15 cm x 15 cm)

CUTTING

Cut 1⅛ inch (3 cm) strips of fabric in light and dark colors. You will need about 70 strips of fabric that measure from 1⅛ to 3½ inches (3 cm to 9 cm) in length.

fabric, right side up, on the Roman numeral I location. Sew following the line between X and Roman numeral I. Let the sewing stitches start about ⅟₁₆ inch (1.5 mm) before the line's start, and sew a few stitches, about ⅟₁₆ inch (1.5 mm) beyond the line's end. You do not need to fasten the thread. Remove the sewn pieces from the sewing machine, finger press the seam, and trim the seam allowance. Use an iron to make a flatter pressed seam. Continue by placing a fabric scrap in the Roman numeral II location, and sew in the same manner.

The logic behind this pattern is as follows: X is a red-colored fabric – the center of the block. Roman numerals designate where to use fabrics with light colors, and the spaces with regular numbers designate where to use fabrics with dark colors. The numbers from both systems indicate the seams' sewing sequences.

ASSEMBLE THE PIECES

Scissors bag

Sew together four Log Cabin blocks to make a square. Place the block over thin, cotton batting, and quilt without a backing. Measure your block, and cut out a piece of fabric of the same size. This will be the bag's lining. Place this piece of fabric on the same type of batting as the one that you used for the Log Cabin square, and quilt as you quilted the Log Cabin square. Another option is to use the thinnest synthetic, iron-on batting that you can find. You do not have to do any quilting if you choose this kind of a batting.

Sew the quilted square and the quilted lining fabric together to make two tubes. They are not joined.

Prepare the strap: Sew the strap in place along with the two tubes when they are sewn together at the bag's top edge. Pin the strap ends onto the Log Cabin tube's sides, just above the tube's top edge, and between the two quilted tubes that have been placed over each other with right sides facing. You should see only a little of the strap's ends at the top of the bag where you will be sewing.

FINISH IN STYLE

Hand stitch the two tubes together at the top of the bag. If you want to use a sewing machine, just be aware that it will be tight and hard to get to the place where you want to sew. Sew together the bottom of the Log Cabin tube. Turn the bag inside out and press. Sew the lining's bottom together by hand.

PINCUSHION

The pincushion is completely flat. It is made up of one Log Cabin block, batting, and backing. Sandwich the block, batting, and backing, and sew three and a half sides together with right sides facing. Use the small opening to turn the pincushion inside out. Make sure to fasten your thread well at the beginning and at the end of the seam. You may want to sew some small "fake bottom" corners at all four corners to give the pincushion a little height. Trim the seam allowances, especially at the corners. Turn the pincushion inside out, press, and sew the opening shut. Finish off by quilting. You can use the quilting seams to sew the opening shut. Use Quilters Dream Supreme batting for the batting to create a little height.

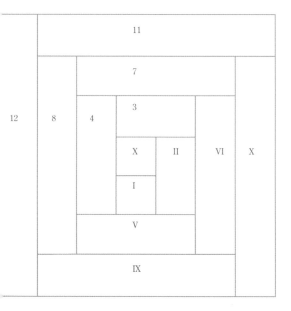

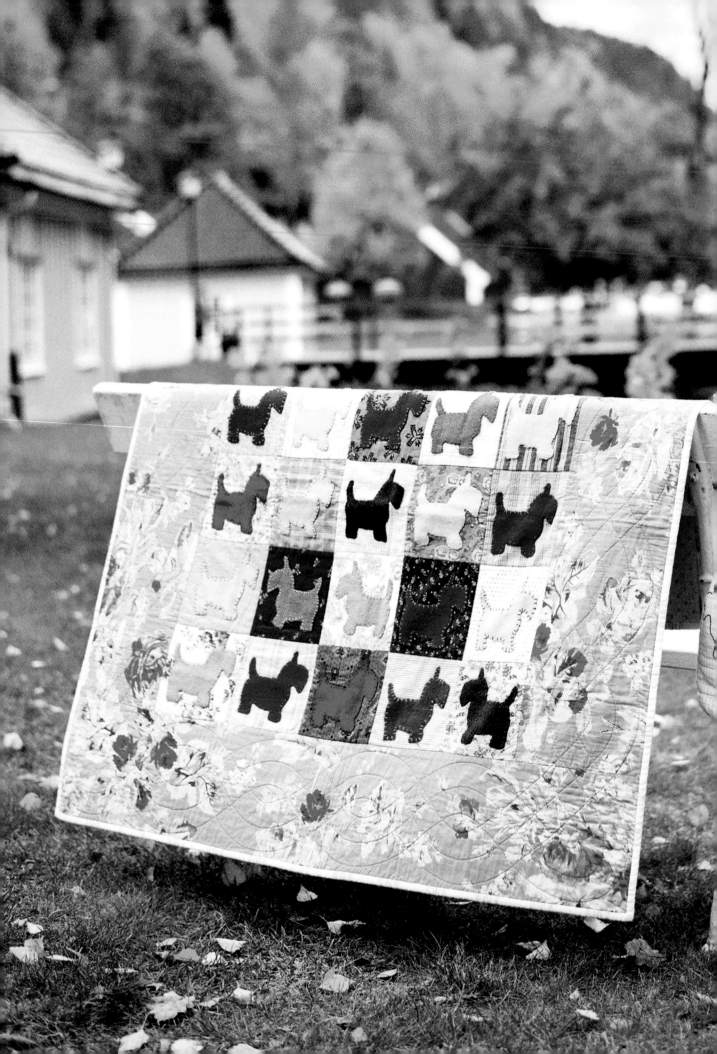

Part Two:
Quilt Making

CHAPTER 4 Simple Bed-size Quilts
"Four Square" Chirp-chirp Quilt
"Four Square" Red Checkerboard Quilt
"Brick Wall" Summer Quilt
Warm Winter Quilt
Embroidered Wool Quilt
Starry Night Quilt with Appliqué

CHAPTER 5 For the Experienced Quilter
Grandmother's Flower Garden
Ohio Star
Memories of Provence
Clamshell Quilt
Blue Dog Quilt
Grandmother's Garden
Cauliflower Soup

CHAPTER 6 Trine's "Encyclopedia" of Tips & Tricks

CHAPTER 4
Simple Bed-size Quilts

A few of the projects in the previous chapter gave you an idea of how to quilt, how to use batting, and how to use backing. Now, we'll move on to larger sizes of projects. You'll soon see that I often recommend sending your assembled quilt to a professional sewer who may have the equipment to finish it smoothly and in style. But of course, you may choose to hand sew your quilt (I provide directions in Chapter 6 if you want to go that route.)

As a beginner, choose cotton fabrics of similar thicknesses, and without any stretch. If you are going to buy rulers to use for cutting fabric pieces, choose one with measurements in inches. I think that the most inspiring projects that I have seen have been based on inch measurements. If you already own a centimeter ruler, it will also work.

Make sure to pay attention to the pattern author's seam allowance size when you are sewing. If the pattern is composed of several different geometric shapes, it becomes especially important to make sure that you have the right seam allowance sizes. In this book, I use a $\frac{3}{8}$-inch (1 cm) seam allowance. Projects that are sewn using a sewing machine require that you keep an even seam allowance everywhere. I recommend that you sew slowly, and use many pins to keep the fabrics in place. See Chapter 6 for hand stitching instructions. Both methods are equally useful.

Patterns are included at the back of the book, but you can get ready-to-use templates for the projects that feature hexagons, stars, etc. They will help you make all the shapes an identical size.

"Four Square"
Chirp-chirp Quilt

FINISHED SIZE
About 65 x 52¾ inches (165 cm x 134 cm)

MATERIALS
- wool fleece for the backing, about 67 x 55 inches (170 cm x 140 cm)
- about 15 inches (38 cm) of 45-inch wide fabric for binding strip
- about 69 inches (175 cm) of fabric for the border
- about 44 inches (112 cm) of background fabric for the squares (71 squares)
- about 44 inches (112 cm) of fabric scraps for the other squares (72 squares)

CUTTING
Cut all 143 squares the same size: 4½ x 4½ inches (11.5 cm x 11.5 cm).

Cut the border 6⅞ inches (17.5 cm) wide on the long sides and 9 inches (23 cm) wide on the short sides.

This project is a good one to begin with if this is your first bed-size quilt. It has a very simple yet pleasing composition and pretty much guarantees success. Start by choosing two fabrics that enhance and complement each other. One of the fabrics will be the border around the quilt, and the other one will be used in every other square as background fabric throughout the quilt. If desired, use fabric scraps for all the other squares.

DESIGN AND STITCHING | **TRINE BAKKE**

QUILTING | **MERETE ELLINGSEN**

BEGIN
Sew rows of squares together. I think it looks best if you start and stop each row with squares of the same type of fabric, either background fabric or scrap fabric squares. Start and finish every other row with background fabric squares, and do the same with the scrap fabric squares. Always iron the seam allowances toward the scrap fabric squares. Sew the rows together. Pin the fabric squares together where they meet at the corners. Sew together 11 squares for each row, and then 13 rows together, adding up to a total of 143 squares.

ASSEMBLE THE PIECES
Sew borders around the assembled squares. First attach a short border piece to each of the quilt top's two short sides, and then sew one long border piece onto each of the two long sides.

FINISH IN STYLE
Place the quilt top on top of the backing – in this case, a piece of wool fleece. (Be sure you have washed the fleece on a wool setting in the washing machine and that you use this temperature setting for any future laundering.)

The assembled piece was quilted by a professional with a large quilting machine, and the bias tape binding strip was added at the end, after quilting.

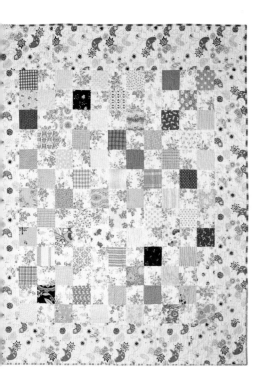

"Four Square" Red Checkerboard Quilt

FINISHED SIZE
About 47 x 87 inches (120 cm x 220 cm) washed and tumbled dry

MATERIALS
- about 47 inches (120 cm) of light-colored for non-red squares (94 squares)
- medium and dark red fabric scraps in a wide variety of reds, smallest usable size is 4¾ x 4¾ inches (12 cm x 12 cm) (95 squares)
- about 17¾ inches (45 cm) of light, striped fabric for the narrow border
- about 55⅛ inches (140 cm) of red-and-white checkerboard fabric for the wide border
- about ½ yard (46 cm) of 45-inch wide fabric for binding strip
- about 55⅛ x 94½ inches (140 cm x 240 cm) for batting
- about 55⅛ x 94½ inches (140 cm x 240 cm) fabric for backing

CUTTING
The seam allowance is ⅜ inch (1 cm).

Cut 94 light-colored fabric squares measuring 4¼ x 4¼ inches (11 cm x 11 cm) each.

Cut 95 fabric squares in a variety of red colors measuring 4¼ x 4¼ inches (11 cm x 11 cm) each.

Cut the light-colored fabric border 2¾ inches (7 cm) wide.

Cut the red-and-white checkerboard fabric border 7 inches (18 cm) wide.

I love the dominant reds in this piece, but I'd like you to notice how the light-colored, inside border gives the quilt "room to breathe," so that the piece doesn't look too chaotic and congested. I often use "breathing borders" to enhance a quilt's appearance. With this project, we'll move into adding the "puffy" layer, the batting.

DESIGN AND STITCHING | **TRINE BAKKE**

BEGIN
Sew rows of nine squares together, alternating every other red and white square. Eleven of the rows begin and end with a red square, and the other ten rows begin and end with a white square. Press all the seam allowances at once, and always toward the red fabric.

ASSEMBLE THE PIECES
Sew all the rows together to make the quilt's center. Pin the quilt's pieces together making sure that all the corners meet. First sew the light-colored border pieces onto the checkerboard's long sides, and then add the same fabric borders onto the short sides. Measure the quilt at the center, and pull or push at the center area as necessary to make sure that the quilt has the same dimensions everywhere. Repeat the same procedure for the red-and-white checkerboard fabric border pieces.

FINISH IN STYLE
Place the quilt top on top of batting and a backing, baste, and quilt. This quilt has been quilted in all the seams on the white sides, and along the edges. To quilt, use a walking foot and a 4.5 stitch length setting on your sewing machine. Sew slowly, and stay away from the red fabrics. When you have finished quilting, trim the quilt, and add a bias tape at the edges to bind off.

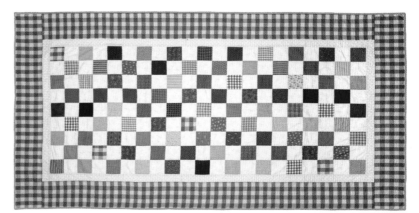

This quilt is double sided and has decorative X-shaped ties in red Pearl embroidery thread that match the red binding strip. The quilt's different blocks are composed of all kinds of fabrics – from jeans to linen, and the colors are blue, green, turquoise, brown, and neutral linen colors in various hues and saturations. My color recipe is simple to remember: Choose block colors that are a little "related to each other" and you can't go wrong. Then choose a binding strip color that is totally different from these colors, and use this same color for the X-shaped ties that hold the quilt layers together.

"Brick Wall" Summer Quilt

(see matching "Brick Wall" Bolster with Appliqué on page 33)

FINISHED SIZE
About 56¼ x 81½ inches (143 cm x 207 cm)

MATERIALS
- 15¾ inches (40 cm) each from 15 different fabrics to make 96 rectangles for the quilt top
- 15 pieces of fabric for the hexagons used on the backing (all from different fabrics), 4 x 4 inches (10 cm x 10 cm). One of the hexagon fabrics should be a red color that works well with the binding strip and Pearl embroidery thread colors.
- 3.5 yards (3.2 m) light gray, checkered fabric for the backing
- ½ yard of 45-inch wide red, checkered fabric for the binding strip
- red-orange Pearl embroidery thread
- 1½-inch (3.8 cm) ready-made templates or templates made by cutting 1½-inch (3.8 cm) hexagons from pattern paper
- Quilters Dream Request cotton batting in queen size
- appliqué thread

CUTTING
All 96 brick pieces were cut exactly the same size as our ruler, 14⅛ x 4¼ inches (36 cm x 11 cm).

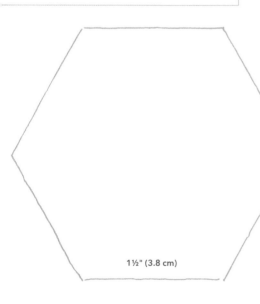

1½" (3.8 cm)

BEGIN
We used a total of 15 different fabrics for this quilt and cut seven pieces from each, ending up with 105 fabric pieces. Since we only need 96 fabric pieces for this quilt, we had nine left over. We put eight of them to good use to make the "Brick Wall" Bolster with Appliqué on page 33.

If you have the space, lay all your pieces on the floor in a Brick Wall (or Wooden Log) pattern so there are six pieces wide and 16 pieces high. Place the various colors and patterns in such a manner that the overall result is harmonious and dynamic. Do not, for example, place a group of brown pieces in one corner, but spread the color out evenly throughout the quilt top.

ASSEMBLE THE PIECES
When you have finished placing the bricks in a pleasing pattern, mark each piece with a piece of paper so that you know each brick's exact location as you sew them together. Sew together rows of six horizontal pieces. Next, sew the rows together until you have 16 rows. Press the seam allowances alternatively to the left and the right on the different rows. This makes it easier to pin the rows together exactly at the meeting points/seams.

FINISH IN STYLE
Backing
The quilt top's backing was sewn from a variety of leftover fabric pieces. We chose fabric pieces of different sizes in light gray colors. The quilt's backing should be relatively neutral in color, and the color should work well with the machine quilting thread's color that will be used for the quilt. Make the back side about 8 inches (20 cm) larger than the quilt top. This will make the process easier when you sandwich the batting between the quilt top and the backing.

Place the quilt top on top of the batting. We chose a thin cotton batting that is easy to quilt by hand or by sewing machine. Cut the batting the same size as the quilt's backing. Place the backing with the right side down, then the batting, and then the quilt top, with the right side up, on the top. Baste all the layers together either by sewing or by using basting spray.

Machine quilting
Sew with a 4.5 stitch length setting on your sewing machine. Try to sew evenly in the ditch, or at least within 1/16 inch (1.5 mm) inside the seam where the seam allowance does not lie. Fasten the thread well at the beginning and at the end of the seams. Trim the quilted quilt so that the batting and the backing are exactly the same size as the quilt top.

Hand quilting
By hand, embroider X-shaped ties in the middle of every other fabric piece using red-orange Pearl embroidery thread.

Fasten the thread well. The X should look good on the quilt's front side. On the backing side, appliqué a hexagon over the spot where the embroidery thread shows (thanks to Anne-Kjersti for the idea).

Hexagon appliqués for the backing
Prepare 48 hexagons as described in the instructions for the Indigo Pillow with Hexagons (page 30). Appliqué the hexagons onto the quilt's backing by using invisible appliqué stitches. Choose an appliqué thread color that matches the hexagon's fabric color.

Warm Winter Quilt

FINISHED SIZE
About 54¼ x 36⅝ inches (138 cm x 93 cm) washed at a wool setting and tumbled dry on a low temperature

MATERIALS
- 24 flannel pieces of various colors, 10 x 10 inches (25 cm x 25 cm) each
- fabric for the batting, 59⅛ x 39⅜ inches (150 cm x 100 cm)
- fabric for the backing, 59⅛ x 39⅜ inches (150 cm x 100 cm)
- 13 inches (33 cm) of 45-inch wide fabric in a fun color for the binding strip

CUTTING
Cut 24 10 x 10 squares

This quilt is a delightful project to work on. Wool flannel (or worsted flannel), which I've used here, makes this quilt softer, cozier, and with more loft than wool. If you use somewhat equal-sized fabric squares in muted, harmonious colors, and a binding strip in a contrasting color, you will give this piece "that little extra" that will keep it from becoming boring.

DESIGN AND STITCHING | **TRINE BAKKE**

BEGIN
Sew together four squares to make a row, and make six rows. Then sew the rows together to make a quilt top.

ASSEMBLE THE PIECES
Place the quilt top on top of batting and backing, with the wrong sides toward the batting. Baste the layers together and quilt. The quilt shown uses a quilting pattern with parallel, vertical lines.

FINISH IN STYLE
Use a binding strip in a contrasting color to enliven the quilt.

Embroidered Wool Quilt

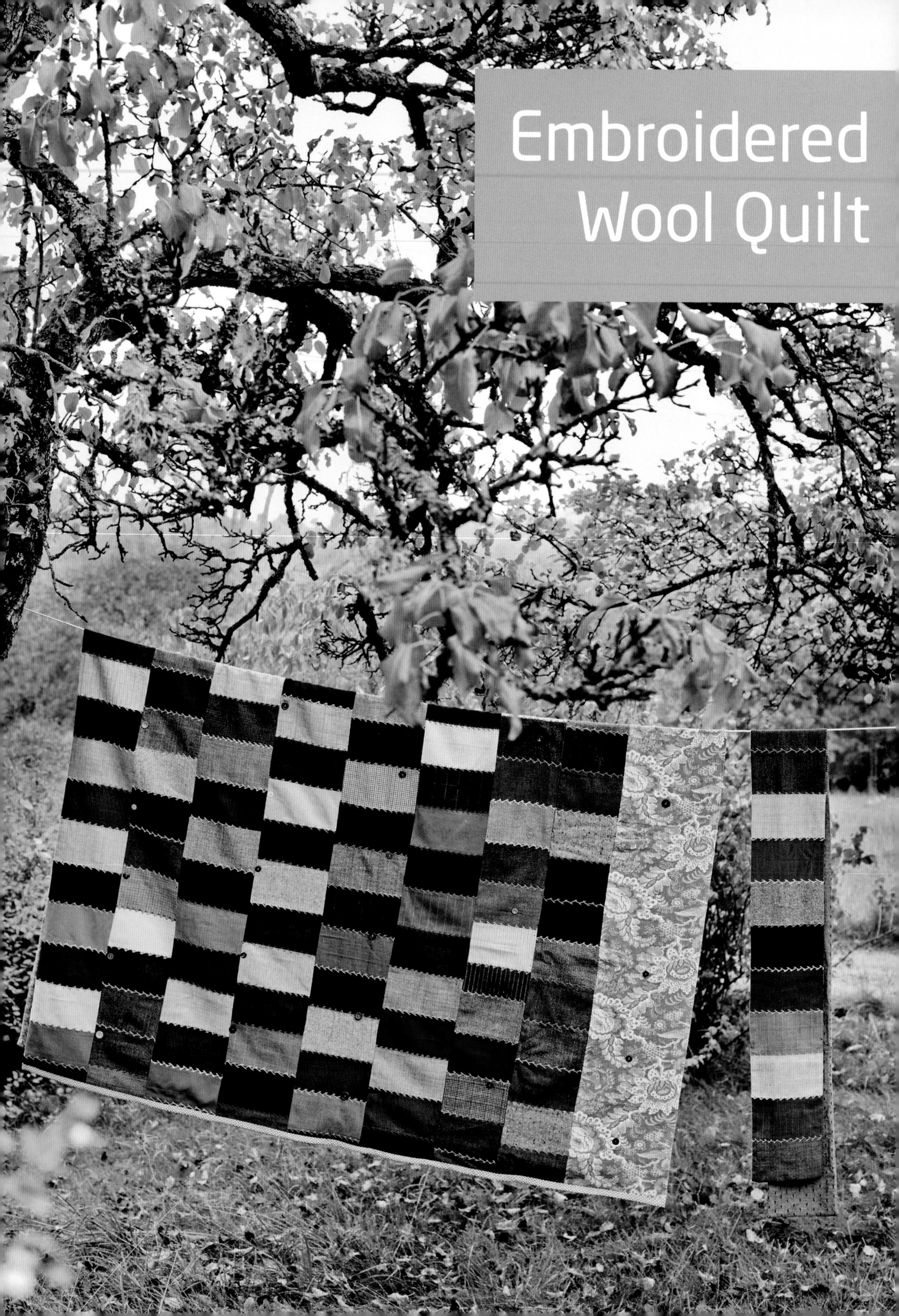

FINISHED SIZE
About 63 x 86½ inches (160 cm x 220 cm)

MATERIALS
- wool fabric scraps, measuring from about 6¼ x 4¾ inches (16 cm x 12 cm)
- 51 buttons with a ⅜- to 1-inch (1 cm to 2.5 cm) diameter in a variety of colors
- several skeins of embroidery thread
- 19 inches (23 cm) of 45-inch wide fabric for binding strip
- 67 inches (170 cm) linen fabric for the tube backing
- 67 inches (170 cm) cotton fabric for the tube backing

CUTTING
The width and length of each patch varies slightly. The lengths can be any size from 6¼ inches (16 cm) to 8⅛ inches (20.5 cm) long, but the widths are more even in size, around 4½ inches (11.5 cm) to 4¾ inches (12 cm) wide.

This quilt has been made from fabric samples meant for wool suits that have been taken out of sample books. You can still see the holes in some of the fabrics where they were attached to the salesmen's binders. Each horizontal seam has been decorated with colorful embroideries. The quilt was assembled using a total of 178 small wool sample patches. See the matching Wool Scarf with Embroidery, which is made from leftover patches, on page 15.

DESIGN AND STITCHING | TRINE BAKKE

OVERVIEW
The pieces of wool are approximately the same size and have been sewn together in rows. Each row has about 22 rectangular patches, and the quilt is composed of eight rows. The seam allowances have been pressed open, and each row has been embroidered at the seam between two different patches, before the rows were sewn together. We chose many different thread colors for the embroideries. A cotton Pearl thread will work very well. Then, we sewed all the rows together to make the quilt top and trimmed the rows, to make sure that all the rows were equally long.

ASSEMBLE THE PIECES/SEW A TUBE
Sew the two fabric pieces for the quilt's backing together to make one piece. The backing must be at least as long as the trimmed quilt top, and about 17¼ inches (44 cm) wider. I have used a piece of somewhat heavy linen and a light cotton fabric for the backing. Half of the linen fabric's width will show on the quilt's front side when the quilt has been finished. See the photo of the full quilt on page 116.

Sew the backing and the quilt top together along the long edges, right sides facing. Since the backing is larger than the quilt top, it will not lie flat against the quilt top, but bunch in the middle. I call this technique to sew "a pipe" or "a tube" (see page 115). Press the seams and turn "the tube" inside out.

FINISH IN STYLE
Place the tube flat on a surface with the right side facing out. I chose to let 8⅝ inches (22 cm) of the backing fabric be visible on the front of the quilt, so that it became something of a border.

Pin safety pins through both fabric layers where you will be sewing on buttons. I used a book as a measurement template to find out how closely I wanted to space the safety pins. Next, sew on a button through both layers where you have placed a safety pin. Remove the safety pin, and continue to sew on buttons at all the other locations where you have placed safety pins. The buttons will act as quilting, or "that which holds the layers in place." I went through my button collection and sorted out all the buttons that were about ⅜ to 1 inch (1 cm to 2.5 cm) in diameter and used them for this project.

The quilt's short edges have been trimmed with bias tape in a contrasting color.

SEWING WITH WOOL
Wool fabrics are often looser and have a less stable weave than tightly woven cotton fabrics. It is a good idea, when sewing with wool, to place the pins closely together, and to sew with a wider seam allowance than you would normally use.

Starry Night Quilt with Appliquéd Bolster

FINISHED SIZE
About 61¾ x 56⅝ inches (157 cm x 144 cm)

MATERIALS
- 37⅜ inches (95 cm) blue stars heavyweight cotton fabric for every other rectangle
- 25⅝ inches (65 cm) brown wool fabric for every other rectangle
- about 19 inches (23 cm) of 45-inch wide for two edges measuring 45 inches (115 cm). Add an inch or two for turning corners.
- 12 green buttons
- backing and front border fabrics, 61¾ x 56⅝ inches (157 cm x 144 cm); I used wool, a tablecloth and denim fabrics for the backing
- a ruler with cutting dimensions of 6 x 12 inches (15 cm x 30 cm)
- a piece of fabric for the back of the pillow (I used the wool from an old buttoned blazer), 13 x 23⅝ inches (33 cm x 60 cm) with the placket buttoned

CUTTING
For the blanket, cut 13 blue and 12 brown rectangles, each measuring 6 x 12 inches (15 cm x 30 cm). Cut out two extra rectangles from each color for the pillow.

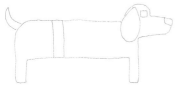

See the pattern on page 119.

This blanket has been sewn using a combination of heavyweight cotton and a similar weight of wool for the rectangles.

DESIGN AND STITCHING | **TRINE BAKKE**

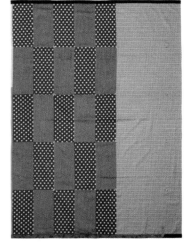

BEGIN
Sew the blue cotton and brown wool rectangles together to make a quilt top using a five-by-five grid.

BACKING
Sew the large piece of wool and the tablecloth together along a long edge. The backing fabric and border piece are sewn together to make one piece of fabric that measures 61¾ x 56⅝ inches (157 cm x 144 cm). The different fabrics for the backing are cut in this way: the wool fabric (for the front border and parts of the backing) is cut to 37 (94 cm) wide x 56⅝ inches (144 cm) long, the tablecloth is cut to 25⅝ (65 cm) wide x 35⅜ inches (90 cm) long, and the denim fabric is cut to 25⅝ (65 cm) wide x 21⅝ inches (55 cm) long. You sew the denim fabric together with the tablecloth to make a piece that measures 56⅝ inches (144 cm) in width.

ASSEMBLE THE PIECES AND FINISH IN STYLE

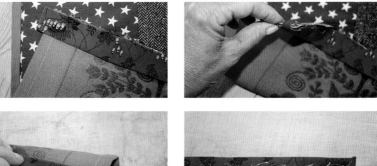

Assemble the pieces as described on page 71. Make a tube from the quilt top and pieced backing by sewing them together along the long sides, right sides facing. Turn the project inside out and place it flat on a surface. Fasten the two layers together by sewing buttons through the layers, and trim the blanket's short edges with bias tape to finish. For more finishing instructions, see page 113.

SEW A PILLOW FROM THE LEFTOVERS
Take the four leftover rectangles (that you cut out with all the other rectangles). Sew the pieces together and appliqué a dog on top. I cut out my dog by freehand while looking at a drawing of a dog on a lunch box. The dog has been appliquéd to the pillow's front with raw edges and rough stitches. You may want to use fusible webbing and blanket stitches for the appliqué. The pillow is finished as described on page 16, "Four Patch" Wool Bolster.

CHAPTER 5
For the Experienced Quilter

The cutting and sewing in the patterns in this chapter are technically more challenging, and a bit more interesting, than earlier chapters. I think this is a good thing.

I've never been a fan of ready-made fabric collections such as jelly rolls or layer cakes (although I have been known to use them, even in this book!). My preference is to recycle and reuse fabrics from dresses I loved, handsome shirts my husband once wore, vintage linens and wool flannel I've found at yard sales, and – well . . . you get the idea. When it comes to fabric selection, I ask you to challenge yourself to play with several different types of textiles. Choose from a rich selection of cloth with different patterns and colors. Consider fabrics in an array of colors that "bump" into each other and fabrics with patterns that "speak the same language." Don't shy away from large patterns or stripes and checks.

My Theory on Traditional Norwegian Sweaters

What can a traditional knitted Norwegian sweater pattern (Mariusgenser) possibly have to do with color theory and fabric selection? I often compare it to the process of knitting a traditional Norwegian sweater or any pattern that may be "held hostage" by tradition. If your aim is to reproduce a blue sweater with a red-and-white pattern, then you will buy the yarn that is recommended, and knit a sweater that exactly matches the one in the pattern. However, if you want to play with colors, you will make your own yarn color selection and knit a sweater that becomes "yours" alone. Maybe you want to experiment with brown, orange, and light blue, or maybe purple with light blue and mint? Maybe you want to select a gray color as the main color, and choose red and pink for the pattern, or maybe mustard with gray and turquoise?

Think this way as you select your fabrics.

Tools I Love

There are always new tools for quilters popping up in the marketplace. Some of these are indispensible, while others are easy to live without. Keep track of the new products by checking in with your local quilting groups or online, or by going to your local hobby store. Here are three products that I really like and recommend.

Quilt Basting Spray: This product does away with hand basting, safety pins, and quilt basting gun fasteners that you may have been using to secure your quilt top to the batting. Use a thin spray, and cover the area around your work.

Fabric Glue Basting Pen: Use as a substitute for hand basting and paper clips when doing English paper piecing (EPP). Use a thin line, and be sure to avoid the outer edges of the fabric where you will be sewing.

Paper Piece Packs and Templates: There is a large selection of many different template shapes that you can purchase, and they can make hand stitching a perpetual trip through new patterns. Paper Pieces and Sue Daley have many different shapes to choose from.

Ready, set, get inspired!

Grandmother's Flower Garden

FINISHED SIZE
About 65 x 81 inches (165 cm x 206 cm)

MATERIALS
- 1¼-inch (3 cm) ready-made hexagon templates from Sue Daley or Paper Pieces, or 1¾-inch (4.4 cm) templates made from plastic or cardboard (seam allowance included)
- fabric for 40 different flowers with different centers; all together, 80 different fabrics about 12 x 10 inches (30 cm x 25 cm) each (40 of the fabrics can be smaller because they are used only for the flower centers)
- 3.3 yards (3 m) light-colored fabric for the sashing and background flowers
- 23¾ inches (60 cm) fabric for the centers of the background flowers
- 2 yards (1.8 m) fabric for border
- 19 inches (49 cm) of 45-inch wide for binding strip
- 2 yards (1.8m) fabric for backing
- for the batting, a piece about 69 x 85 inches (175 cm x 216 cm)

CUTTING
Trace the pattern and cut out the fabric hexagons. Use a 1¾-inch (4.4 cm) template of your choice to trace the cutting lines onto the fabric. When you have traced one hexagon onto the fabric, place the template, again, on the fabric right next to the one that you have already drawn to create a honeycomb design. The cutting lines will then line up. You will save a lot of fabric by using this method, especially when you are cutting the fabric for the background flowers. Use a marker for tracing the lines onto the fabric that will not run or bleed through your fabric. Cut out hexagons precisely by following the drawn lines, and use a pair of sharp scissors.

Tip
Place the quilt top on top of batting and backing, with the wrong sides towards the batting. Baste the layers together and quilt. Add binding strip.

The photographs on pages 61 and 78-79 show this quilt design in different palettes. The first uses cool colors while the next one is warm. Both have been sewn using the same hexagon pattern. The color selections really make a difference!

DESIGN AND STITCHING | **TRINE BAKKE, ANNE-KJERSTI JOHANSEN, AND ANNE FJELLVÆR**

BEGIN
Tack the fabric pieces onto the ready-made templates, and sew the fabric-covered hexagons together. See the instructions on page 100, Cauliflower Soup. Sew 40 flowers in different colors, then make 52 background flowers with a colored hexagon "dot" in the middle.

ASSEMBLE THE PIECES
Place the 40 flowers in eight rows with five hexagon flowers in each row. Sew them together with the background flowers, and use the same light-colored fabric for sashing. Refer to the photos and drawings for help.

Trim the hexagon pattern pieces so that you get straight edges at the quilt's edges, and 90 degrees at the corners. Sew the modified hexagons together as instructed above. Add a border around the flowers using either the hand-stitched or machine-stitched instructions below.

HAND-STITCHED BORDER
Decide how wide you want the quilt's border to be, and cut freezer paper to that size. Measure your quilt to get the right lengths. Choose a fabric and cut out the border pieces including seam allowances. Press the freezer paper's waxy side onto the wrong side of the fabric, and baste the fabric border pieces in place with the seam allowances folded toward the paper side. Attach the border pieces to the quilt by hand stitching, starting with the long sides first, and then adding the short sides.

MACHINE-STITCHED BORDER
Make sure that all the modified hexagons' seam allowances, at the quilt's edges, are left flat with the seam allowances pressed toward the outside. Finish the background areas by hand stitching.

Draw the seam allowances at the modified hexagon edges in this way: Following the template pieces' edges on the wrong side of the fabric, draw a line on the fabric with a pencil or tailor's chalk exactly where the template ends. This will be the line that you will sew along when you machine stitch the border pieces in place.

HOW WIDE IS THE BORDER?
The maximum border width is the width of a fabric divided by four. You can choose the minimum width. Take a look at your work and decide which width will work the best.

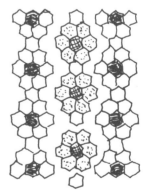

See the photo of the finished quilt on the next page.

FINISHED SIZE
Finished quilt is 55 x 79 inches (140 cm x 200 cm); each finished block sewn in place is 6 x 6 inches (15 cm x 15 cm)

MATERIALS
- 71 inches (180 cm) blue-black background fabric for every other block
- 59 pieces of different light-colored fabric for the star blocks, 10 x 12 inches (25 cm x 30 cm) each
- 59 pieces of different dark-colored fabric for the star blocks, 10 x 12 inches (25 cm x 30 cm) each
- 118 different light and dark fabrics for the 59 star blocks, 10 x 12 inches (25 cm x 30 cm) each
- for the batting, a piece about 59 x 83 inches (150 cm x 211 cm)
- fabric for the backing, about 59 x 83 inches (150 cm x 211 cm)
- ½ yard of 45-inch wide for the binding strip (92 cm)

For hand stitching
- templates in the following sizes: 2-inch (5 cm) square, 6-inch (15 cm) square, 2-inch (5 cm) quarter-square triangle

For machine stitching
- 2½ x 2½-inch (6.5 cm) ruler (optional)
- one roll triangle paper pattern, finished size 2 quarter-square triangles

HELPFUL HINTS
If you sew using centimeters, I have some bad news: The machine sewing instructions noted below will not work with centimeter measurements. Read the whole text before you despair; there is help.

A good alternative is to sew a sample quarter-square on the sewing machine. Choose your own dimensions and make your own drawing on paper. See the instructions under "Machine Stitching" on page 82 to understand the process. When you have sewn the quarter-square, measure it. This measurement is then the answer to what size the small squares should be cut. Now sew a sample star block. When you have completed this block, measure it, and cut the background blocks in the same size. You have now been set free from my pattern to your own.

There is yet another way to do this: If you manage to calculate and make a 5 cm (2 inch) sewn and finished quarter-square, with a 1 cm (⅜ inch) seam allowance, these measurements will work: The square in the star block will be 7 cm x 7 cm (2¾ x 2¾ inches), and the background blocks will be 17 cm x 17 cm (6⅝ x 6⅝ inches). Cut 58 of the large ones.

Star block construction
You need four light squares, one dark square, four quarter-squares with the light and dark color.

Do you sometimes feel like sewing by hand and other times with a sewing machine? Both methods are fully described in the text below. Read the entire text before you make up your mind.

DESIGN AND STITCHING | **TRINE BAKKE**

MACHINE QUILTING | **ANNE RØNNINGEN, QUILTKAMMERET**

HAND STITCHING
Cut out the fabric pieces and be sure to include the seam allowances. Make them as even as possible; the stitching, quilting, and the blocks will look better with even seam allowances. It is, also, a good idea to trim the top off the corner seam allowances after you have sewn. You can use the pink glue pen from Sewline for all your basting. Put a little glue along one of the cut fabric pieces' edge, fold the seam allowance over toward the wrong side of the fabric, press down with your fingers, and hold for a few seconds until the seam allowance stays in place. Another useful method is to stitch the seam allowances in place. Usually, I sew through the fabric and the template, but not everyone does this. I use paper clips to hold the fabric in place until I have basted the seam allowances. Choose a basting thread that is in contrast to your fabric color, so that it will be easy to locate the stitches at the end when you are done, and are going to pull them out. Both the template and the basting stitches should be removed. However, that said, some people choose a neutral thread because they plan to leave the basting stitches in the finished quilt. Also, they do not sew through the template, because it will be removed. You will find your own method; just remember to wait to remove the templates until all the seams around a fabric-wrapped template have been sewn onto another template.

Take two already-basted pieces and place one on top of the other, with right sides facing. Stitch them together along the edges. Carefully poke the needle through the fabric edges of both pieces, catching a few fabric threads; do not sew into the templates. Make sure to securely fasten your thread at the beginning and end of each seam. Use a sharp, thin needle and a good-quality thread for the stitching. My needle is so very thin, and the eye so very small, that I have become dependent upon a needle threader. Place another basted piece in place next to the others, and repeat the process. As the block grows, you will have to fold some basted pieces in the middle to be able to place them right sides facing each other. That is not a problem.

Sew four triangles, two of each color, together to make a four square. I find it easiest to sew two triangles together first, then add the third one. The fourth triangle is added last. So, do not sew two and two triangles together to make four, but sew two together + the third + the fourth. Sew four squares, so that each is made up of four triangles. Make the star by sewing nine squares together in the right order. Note that the center square is always surrounded by triangles that have been made from a different fabric.

You can remove the templates as you go and reuse them for new star blocks; just don't remove a template that does not have a "neighbor." It is best to remove a few of the templates in each star block, leaving the ones at the edges until you have stitched the background blocks in place. The background blocks make up every other block.

Sew the blocks together as you go, making rows with alternating star blocks and background blocks. When you have completed all the rows, sew them together to make a quilt top.

Tips

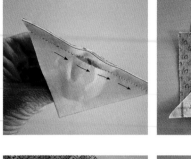

When you are ready to attach the binding/edging strips at the end of your project, you will need a seam allowance at the edge of the quilt to attach the binding strip to. It is, therefore, important to leave the blocks' seam allowances at quilt's edges flat. Make sure that these seam allowances are not basted onto any other seam allowances. Fasten the sewing threads in such a manner that you can place the seam allowances flat at all the quilt's edges.

HOW TO KEEP THE POINTS INTACT

Precisely wrap the fabric around the template, paying attention to the points. "Respect" the template, and do not manipulate it into a shape that it does not have. Keep your touch soft, but firm. When you are basting, complete the shape all the way out to the points. When placing pieces together for stitching, check to make sure that you have template against template. There should be no space against the template, or fabric against template. What you want is the "feeling" of template against template between the fabrics. Check and make sure that both your seam's starting point and ending point are exactly at the template's starting and ending point. Start by sewing from the middle of where the triangles meet the square. Sew an entire sample block to check if you are able to get the points right, before you start sewing to "mass-produce" parts for the blocks.

MACHINE STITCHING

Use a ¼-inch (6 mm) presser foot for your sewing machine; this will help you to sew with an exact ¼-inch (6 mm) seam allowance. Exception: Sew with a slightly less than ¼-inch (6 mm) seam allowance when you sew the quarter-squares. Otherwise, follow the lines on the triangle paper templates. Press the first quarter-square seam allowances toward the dark side, and press the second seam open. Trim the seam allowances at the corners.

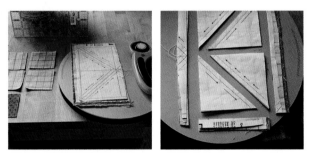

There are rulers available that are exactly 6½ x 6½ inches and 2½ x 2½ inches that you can use for this project.

STAR CONSTRUCTION

Cut a piece off the roll with paper triangle templates, making sure that you have two complete paper triangles. You will need some "air" around these triangles, so you will be ruining the shapes that surround the triangles when you cut them out; that is not a problem because there are more than enough triangles left on the roll for your project. Press two pieces of fabric together with an iron, right sides facing. Attach a paper triangle template with pins onto the wrong side of one fabric, while the fabrics remain pressed together. Trim the fabrics roughly around the paper template. Before you start to cut, remember that you need to have enough fabric to cut four 2½ x 2½ inch (6.4 cm) squares for the star, and one square of the same size for the center of the star. Sew through the paper and both of the fabrics at the same time. Sew on all the stippled lines with a stitch setting of 2, that is, tightly spaced stitches. Use a rotary cutter or scissors to cut along all the solid lines.

Pull off the paper template by holding on to one of the fabric's points and in the middle of the triangle's long side under the seam. Pull quickly with determination from the middle of the long side. Remove the rest of the paper.

Place two and two quarter-squares on top of each other, with the light part over the dark part. Make sure that the seams meet exactly. Rub them together. Draw a diagonal line using a ruler and a pencil. Make sure to hit the shape's points. Sew on each side of the diagonal line, using a ¼-inch (6 mm) seam allowance. You may want to draw a guide line on your sewing machine to locate where the center is. Use this line to guide your sewing.

Cut along the fabric's center line, and fold out the quarter-square. Press the seam apart, and trim the seam allowances' corners. The star is ready to be assembled.

Prepare four quarter-squares, four background squares, and one center square for each star block. Press the quarter-squares before additional sewing. Iron the quarter-square seam allowances toward the dark fabric side.

Sew the stars together, and make sure that you place the quarter-squares in the right position. A good rule to remember is that all squares should match up with a triangle in another fabric.

The photograph above shows how I pressed open the seam allowances. Gather the pieces, then sew the blocks together in rows. Finish by sewing the rows together to make a quilt top.

TIPS ON HOW TO KEEP THE TRIANGLE POINTS INTACT

Use a ¼ inch (6 mm) seam allowance. You must keep this seam allowance completely even everywhere, throughout the entire process. There is no room for seam imperfections. It can be challenging to keep the seam allowance even, especially beginning and at the end of the seam. The seam's first and last ⅛ inch (3 mm) are the most important parts of the seam, and there you must make sure that you are sewing with precisely a ¼-inch (6 mm) seam allowance. You may want to use a pin or a small awl to keep the fabric pieces together while you start and stop sewing.

Place pins in all the seam points that will meet. There are good pins available that are thin, so that you can sew over them with your machine. The pinheads should be made out of glass; that makes it easy to iron the fabric with them in place, and the heads will not melt and damage your fabric.

All the pieces should be placed exactly on top of each other when you sew them together. If one piece is too small or too big, you need to find out why and correct the problem. The solution is not to allow even a tiny mistake to get by you. Due to the pattern's angles and all its points, a mistake will expand and grow as you put the pieces together.

Measure your star blocks before you cut the background blocks. You may have to adjust the size of the background blocks to match the size of the star blocks.

FINISH IN STYLE

Place the quilt top on top of batting and backing, with the wrong sides towards the batting. Baste the layers together and quilt. Add binding strip.

INTACT POINTS

Everyone has their tolerance level when it comes to "intact points." These instructions have given you some pointers. If you want additional information, you may want to check with your stitching friends, search YouTube for "accurate points in machine piecing," ask people at a sewing store, attend a workshop, or just happily sew. Antique quilts seldom have intact points everywhere, and many are actually quite crooked. So do not feel bad if you do not manage to make perfect stars.

See the next page for a photo of the entire quilt top.

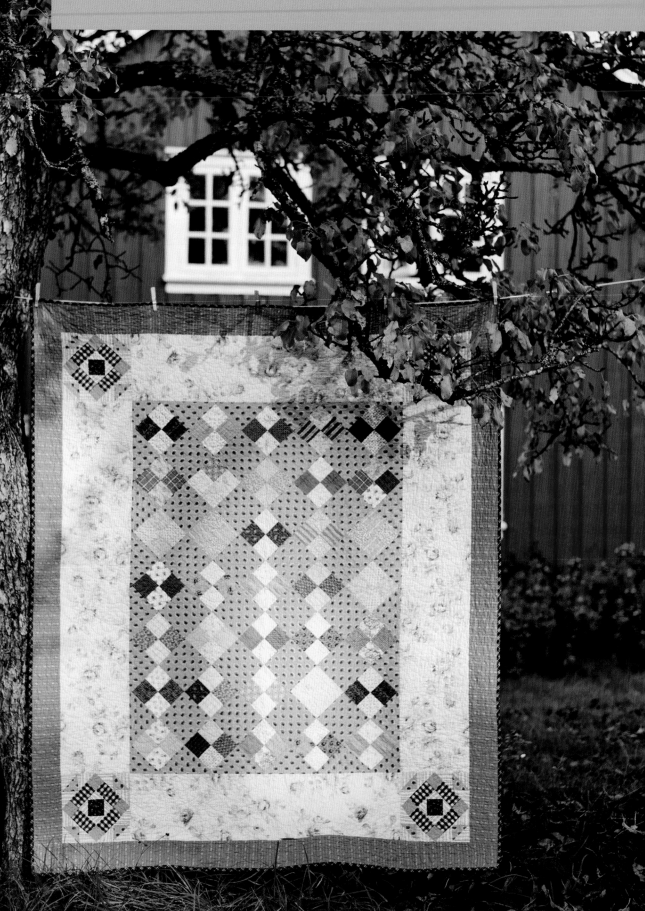

Memories of Provence

FINISHED SIZE
About 57½ x 69¼ inches (146 cm x 176 cm)

BLOCK SIZES
Four Patch: 5 x 5 inches (13 cm x 13 cm)
Jack in the Pulpit: 9 x 9 inches (23 cm x 23 cm)

MATERIALS*
Four Patch: You will use, all together, 1 yard (0.9 m) fabric scraps for the Four Patch blocks. Each piece of fabric can be as small as 4 x 4 inches (10 cm x 10 cm). The fabric colors I have selected are white, yellow, gray, blue, black, and brown. The values go from light to dark. I have used about 50 different fabrics for my Four Patch blocks, that is, 140 pieces for 35 blocks. You will use 70 different fabrics, if you want all the blocks to be different.

Jack in the Pulpit:

- 16 inches (40 cm) striped fabric for the background
- 4 inches (10 cm) blue fabric for the center area
- 8 inches (20 cm) black-and-white check for the rectangles
- 12 inches (30 cm) total of two different yellow fabrics for details

Background fabric:

- 1.6 yards (1.5 m) Provence yellow background fabric
- 1.6 yards (1.5 m) light blue fabric with rose pattern for a border
- 2.2 yards (2 m) blue fabric for the outer border
- ½ yard (50 cm) gray-black fabric for binding strip
- fabric for the backing, about 59 x 63 inches (150 cm x 161 cm)
- piece of batting, about 59 x 63 inches (150 cm x 161 cm)

TIPS FOR CUTTING SIZES
All the measurements are based on a ¼-inch (6 mm) seam allowance. I recommend that you sew a sample block before you cut out all the pieces. It is possible that you will have to increase the size of each piece slightly to keep the points accurate in the Jack in the Pulpit block.

The Jack in the Pulpit dimensions of ⅜ inch (1 cm) and ⅝ inch (1.5 cm) are used to make the block work out mathematically. If you have trouble working with such numbers, you can try to think of them this way:

⅜ inch is a little less than a half (4/8 inch), and is one line below the ½-inch line mark if your ruler has marks for ⅛ inch.

⅝ inch is the same as a little more than a half, and is one line beyond the ½-inch line mark.

Alternatively, you can make hand stitching templates for yourself (see page 88). A finished, sewn Jack in the Pulpit block measures 9 x 9 inches (23 cm x 23 cm).

The inspiration for this quilt was a gift of yellow fabric from a friend who had been in Provence. The deep yellow color represents the brilliant sunflowers and the rich blues are from the area's lavender fields. I added a wide border in a pale, muted color that features a pattern of roses, and finished it with another border of my favorite color, blue.

DESIGN AND STITCHING | **TRINE BAKKE**
MACHINE QUILTING | **ANNE MARIT KNUDSEN**

FOUR PATCH BLOCKS
Cut out 140 fabric pieces that each measure 3 x 3 inches (8 cm x 8 cm) Two sets of two pieces are cut from the same fabric (see photo below).

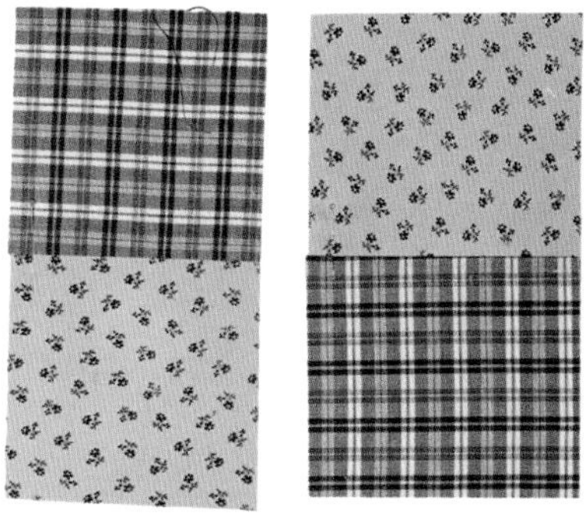

JACK IN THE PULPIT CUTTING SIZES FOR FOUR BLOCKS
Read "Tips for Cutting Sizes" at left.

Striped background fabric: Cut eight fabric squares that each measure 2⅜ x 2⅜ inches (6 cm x 6 cm) and then cut them across diagonally. You will now have 16 triangles (see diagram on next page, B) to use around the blue center square (four in each block). Also cut 24 fabric squares that each measure 3⅛ x 3⅛ inches (8 cm x 8 cm) and then cut them across diagonally. You will now have 48 triangles (see diagram on next page, E) for the block's edges (12 for each block).

Blue fabric for the center squares: Cut four fabric squares that each measure 2¾ x 2¾ inches (7 cm x 7 cm) (see diagram on next page, A) (one for each block).

Black-and-white check rectangles: Cut 16 fabric rectangles at that each measure 2⅛ x 2⅛ inches (5.5 cm x 5.5 cm) (see diagram on next page, C) (four for each block).

Yellow squares: Cut 16 fabric squares 2⅛ inches (see diagram on next page, D) (4 for each block)

Yellow (Provence fabric) outer corners: Cut 8 fabric squares hat each measure 3⅛ x 3⅛ inches (8 cm x 8 cm) and then cut them across diagonally. You will now have 16 triangles (see diagram on next page, E) (four for each block).

*All fabric lengths in the Materials section are based on 45-inch wide fabric.

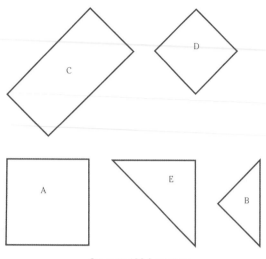

See page 122 for pattern.

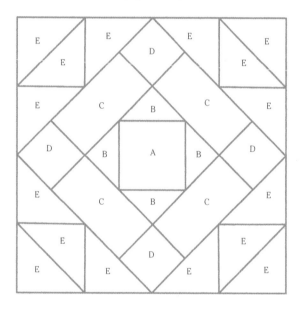

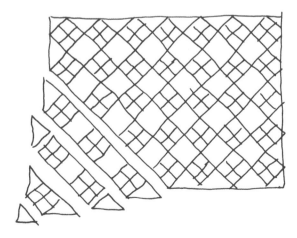

YELLOW PROVENCE FABRIC AS BACKGROUND FABRIC

Cut 24 yellow squares for every other block that each measure 5½ x 5½ inches (14 cm x 14 cm).

Cut two yellow squares that each measure 4½ x 4½ inches (11.4 cm x 11.4 cm) and then cut across diagonally to make four corner triangles.

Cut five yellow squares that each measure 8¼ x 8¼ inches (21 cm x 21 cm) and then cut across diagonally twice to make 20 triangles for the sides.

BORDERS

Light blue fabric with rose pattern:
Cut two borders that each measure 9½ x 35⅞ inches (24 cm x 91 cm).

Cut two borders that each measure 9½ x 50 inches (24 cm x 127 cm).

BORDERS

Cut two borders that each measure 4½ x 68 inches (11.4 cm x 173 cm).

Cut two borders that each measure 4½ x 61 inches (11.4 cm x 155 cm).

BINDING STRIP

½ yard (50 cm) of 45-inch wide gray-black fabric for a binding strip that measures 7.7 yards (7 m) long

BEGIN

Sew the Four Patch blocks, and spread them out – placing them diagonally – so that they create a varied surface pattern. Next, spread out the background blocks that you have cut. Mark the blocks so that you can sew them in the right sequence following the diagonal layout as a sewing plan. Sew diagonal rows, and then sew the rows together to make the quilt's center area.

ASSEMBLE THE PIECES

Sew the four Jack in the Pulpit blocks, and measure a finished block's size. Cut out the light blue fabric with the rose pattern in the same width as the Jack in the Pulpit block. Sew a Jack in the Pulpit block on to each end of the long light blue/rose patterned border pieces. Sew the shorter border lengths onto the quilt top's center area, one on each side. Next sew the long border with a Jack in the Pulpit block at each end onto the quilt top's center area, and then add the blue border in the same way.

FINISH IN STYLE

Place the quilt top on top of batting and a backing, baste, and quilt. Again, I have chosen to let a professional quilter do the quilting. The binding strip is sewn on at the end, when the quilt has been completed and trimmed.

Clamshell Quilt

FINISHED SIZE
38¾ x 32⅞ inches (98.5 cm x 83.5 cm) laundered and tumbled dry

MATERIALS
- 210 different fabric scraps, about 4¾ x 4 inches (12 cm x 10 cm) each
- 4-inch (10 cm) ready-made clamshell templates (from Sue Daley Designs) or templates made by cutting thin card stock or vellum
- fabric for the backing, 42 x 37 inches (107 cm x 94 cm)
- piece of batting, about 42 x 37 inches (107 cm x 94 cm)
- 10 inches (25½ cm) 45-inch wide fabric for binding strip

CUTTING
Cut out 199 clamshells and add seam allowances – be accurate.

From the last 11 fabric scraps, cut out 11 squares measuring 4¾ x 4¾ inches (12 cm x 12 cm) (these measurements assume a ⅜ inch [1 cm] seam allowance); use the squares as a starting point at the top of the quilt.

See page 123 for pattern.

This is a hand-stitched little quilt with clamshell shapes. It has been made from happy fabric scraps that were leftovers from many of my earlier projects. Do as I have done: Cut out clamshell pieces from all the fabrics that pass through your hands over a period of many years. Save them in a box, and glue a clamshell template on the outside of the box so that you know where your stash is. When you have collected enough clamshells, you can start to sew. The quilt will then become a showcase of all the fabrics you have touched.

DESIGN AND STITCHING | TRINE BAKKE

BEGIN
You will be sewing the quilt from the top down. Begin by sewing together a row of 11 fabric squares that will be the background and support for the first row of clamshells. This row of squares will be at the top of your quilt and create a surface for you to appliqué the first clamshells.

PREPARE THE CLAMSHELLS
Baste all the fabric clamshells to your templates, but leave the lower part of the fabric unstitched. It is only the upper, arched part of the clamshell that should be stitched to the template; the lower part should remain unattached. The reason is because that part will be concealed under the next row of clamshell arches when they are appliquéd on top of the previous row.

Piece 10 clamshells together in a long row. Join them with a few stitches right at the points where the arch is at the widest. It is enough to fasten the thread, sew two stitches, and then fasten the thread again.

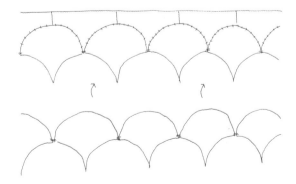

BASTE THE CLAMSHELL ROWS IN PLACE

Place the slightly connected row of clamshells on the starter squares, a little down from the upper edges (see the photograph at right). Take extra care to place the clamshells exactly at the center of the square's seams, and at the same distance from the top. It is easiest to work on a tabletop with some drawn guidelines on the squares, or use anything else that may help you line up the pieces. Baste the whole row of 10 clamshells onto the squares. I like to use pins while the pieces are lying on the table, and afterward to use a sewing machine with a stitch length setting of 6, and to sew two or three seams over the whole row. Remove all the pins, and appliqué the arches. You may want to use glue, basting spray, or plain, old basting stitches instead of my way of doing it. I change the color of my appliqué thread at each arch, so that the thread color matches the clamshell's fabric color. This technique is called invisible hand appliqué.

Sew all the clamshell rows according to the instructions given for the first row. The different rows alternate between rows of 10 or 11 clamshells. You can remove the templates from row two when you start on row four. Continue, in the same manner, to remove the templates as you sew from the top down on the quilt.

ASSEMBLE THE PIECES

Trim all the edges. Make sure to fasten any seam that you may have cut in the process of trimming. I use a sewing machine and some zigzag stitches at the locations where I have messed up a hand-sewn seam. On the other hand, you may want to keep in mind, while you are hand stitching, that you are going to trim your work after you have finished sewing, and consequently, fasten your threads in such a manner that they will not be cut at the end when you trim the quilt top to make it square.

I have not managed to make a squared quilt top and to keep the same sized clamshells at all the edges. You may have more success than I did. It was just when I was almost done with the quilt top that I understood how smart it would have been to have measured and positioned the clamshells more carefully.

FINISH IN STYLE

Sandwich the quilt top on top of batting and a backing. Baste the layers together and quilt. I have used my Sashiko machine, and sewn the quilting seams like an echo pattern over all the clamshells' arches. Trim and sew a bias tape around all the edges.

ALTERNATE SEWING TECHNIQUE

Sew arched seams over the templates. Sue Daley has an instructional video online that will show you this technique.

FINISHED SIZE

About 41⅜ x 41⅜ inches (105 cm x 105 cm) laundered

MATERIALS

- 25 wool fabric scraps, about 5 x 5 inches (12.5 x 12.5 cm) each
- 25 fabric pieces, 6¼ x 6¼ inches (16 cm x 16 cm) each
- cotton Pearl thread for the hand appliqués
- 35½ inches (90 cm) of fabric for the wide borders
- fabric for the backing, 45½ x 45½ inches (115 cm x 115 cm)
- piece of batting, 45½ x 45½ inches (115 cm x 115 cm)
- 10 inches (25 cm) of 45-inch wide fabric for binding strip

CUTTING

Seam allowance is ⅜ inch (1 cm). Cut the border pieces 8 inches (20 cm) wide.

See page 124 for pattern.

Two Norwegian songs from my childhood inspired the Blue Dog Quilt: "I Want a Little Dog" and the other "I Want a Blue Balloon." I mixed these two songs together and made my own version: "I Want a Blue Dog." I sang this song as loudly as possible while swinging wildly on a swing that hung between the pine trees at our cabin in the woods.

DESIGN AND STITCHING | **TRINE BAKKE**

BEGIN

Make a template by tracing the dog template on page 124, and place it on a piece of wool. Hold the template in place, and trace around it using a pencil. Cut out the dog just on the inside of the pencil lines. Fasten the dog shape with pins or by basting it onto a fabric square. The dog's back is located 2½ inches (6.4 cm) from the square's upper edge, the dog's nose is about ¾ inch (2 cm) from the edge, the front paw about 1 inch (2.5 cm), and the back foot about ¾ inch (2 cm) from the edge. Using large stitches, appliqué the dog to the background fabric square.

ASSEMBLE THE PIECES

Repeat this procedure for all the blocks. Make some blocks with a mirrored dog appliqué. Sew the blocks together to make rows, and sew the rows together to make a quilt top. Then sew on the borders.

FINISH IN STYLE

Sandwich the quilt top over batting and a backing. Quilt in the ditch at all the seams, and quilt the borders by following a quilting pattern on Borders Made Easy (see below). Trim and sew on bias tape around all the edges.

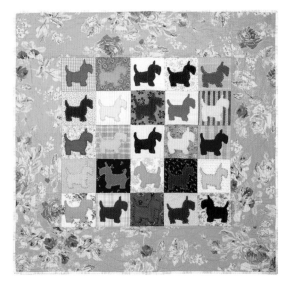

BORDERS MADE EASY

This is a machine quilting aid that has already drawn quilting patterns. You can just make out the quilting pattern on this quilt's borders by looking at the full photograph of the quilt on page 58.

Grandmother's Garden

FINISHED SIZE
About 70 x 56 inches (178 cm x 142 cm)

MATERIALS
- 60 pieces of fabric for the flower petals, 4 x 19¾ inches (10 cm x 50 cm) each
- 60 pieces of fabric for the flower centers, 4 x 4 inches (10 cm x 50 cm) each
- 4 inches (10 cm) of red fabric for the hexagons that fill in the end of the rows
- 1¼-inch (3 cm) ready-made hexagon templates or templates made from cardboard or plastic.
- carrier fabric for the flower appliqués (the red fabric as seen on the photo opposite on the front side of the quilt), is slightly larger at 73 x 62 inches (180 cm x 150 cm)
- piece of fabric for the backing, 71 x 59 inches (180 cm x 150 cm)
- piece of batting (such as Supreme Cotton Batting or wool batting), 71 x 59 inches (180 cm x 150 cm)

An unknown woman, probably from Norway, made this quilt somewhere around 1915 to 1930. I bought it in 2013 from a Norwegian secondhand dealer (who only buys and sells in Norway) at a fair in Hamar, Norway. I have reconstructed the quilt pattern and the sewing instructions. The quilt has 60 hand-stitched hexagon flowers.

DESIGN AND STITCHING | UNKNOWN

BEGIN
This quilt requires 60 hexagon flowers. I recommend going to the Cauliflower Soup quilt on page 101 for instructions on how to sew the flowers.

ASSEMBLE THE PIECES
Use the photograph on pages 98-99 as your guide for how to sew the hexagon flowers together to make a quilt top. They are placed tightly together in a traditional manner. You will make four rows with nine flowers and three rows with eight flowers. Spaces between the flowers on the top and bottom rows are filled in with red hexagons, so the rows are more even.

When all the hexagon flowers have been sewn together into one piece, place them on top of a large carrier piece of fabric, and appliqué in place. This large piece of fabric also becomes the borders around the flowers. The borders will have a serrated look close to the flowers. Next, cut away the fabric under the hexagon flowers.

FINISH IN STYLE
Place your quilt top on top of an extra-thick batting and backing, then quilt in the ditch at all seams. The borders have a simple quilting pattern of parallel lines. Finish the quilt by folding the carrier fabric's extra width and length over to the quilt's back side and sew in place.

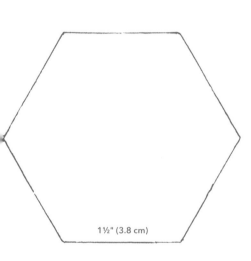

1½" (3.8 cm)

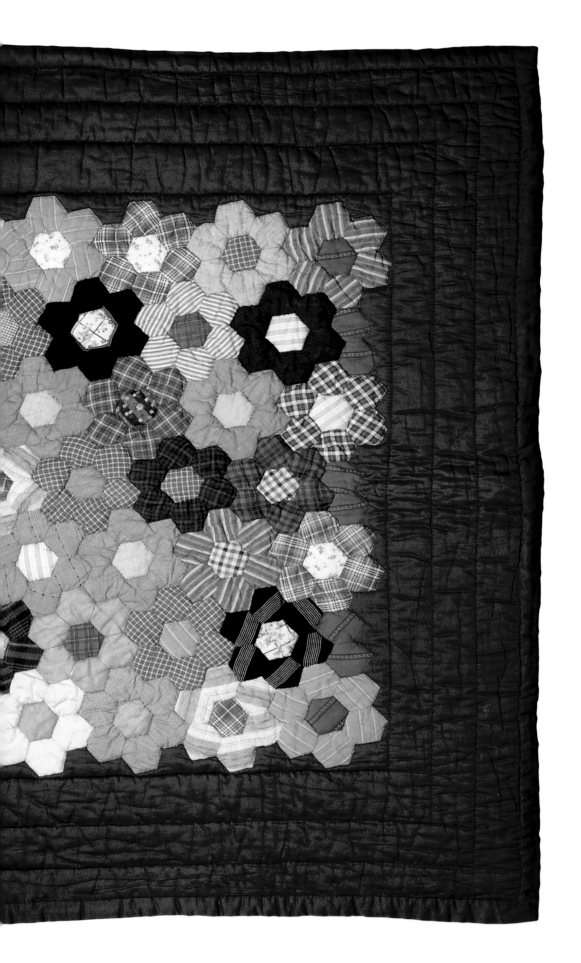

Cauliflower Soup

FINISHED SIZE
About 80⅝ x 55¼ inches (205 cm x 140 cm) quilted and laundered

MATERIALS
- 2-inch (5 cm) hexagon templates
- for each of the 15 blocks:
  6 inches (15 cm) fabric for the hexagon flower petals
  6 inches (15 cm) fabric for the flower's center
  10 inches (25 cm) of two different fabrics for the Four Patch block
- 9 x 9-inch and 15 x 15-inch rulers (optional, but it's much easier to make the blocks if you use the rulers)
- 2.2 yards (2 m) fabric for the borders to create whole border pieces
- piece of fabric for the backing, 94½ x 63 inches (240 cm x 160 cm)
- piece of batting, 94½ x 63 inches (240 cm x 160 cm)
- 19⅝ (50 cm) 45-inch wide for the binding strip

CUTTING
The seam allowance is ⅜ inch (1 cm).

Cut 15 Four Patch blocks for the hexagon flower appliqués. You can use a 7⅞ x 7⅞-inch (20 cm x 20 cm) ruler and cut out two sets of two. Sew together 15 different blocks that have two different pieces of fabric in each, four squares per block.

The borders are 7⅞ inches (20 cm) wide on the sides and 6 inches (15 cm) at the top and bottom.

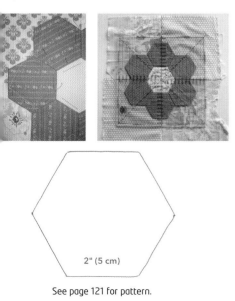

2" (5 cm)

See page 121 for pattern.

A hexagon sewn onto squares is a new take on traditional blocks. Maybe you have a stack of hexagon flowers lying around that have not yet been joined? If that is the case, then you can do as follows: Appliqué the hexagon flowers onto a pieced background. Each block consists of a Four Patch block with a hexagon flower appliqué.

DESIGN AND STITCHING | **TRINE BAKKE AND LINE BAKKE**
QUILTING | **MERETE ELLINGSEN AND LINE BAKKE**

BEGIN
Sew 15 individual hexagon flowers by hand stitching over templates.

Pin a hexagon template onto the fabric's wrong side. Cut out the hexagon adding a seam allowance. Cut evenly and add about ½ inch (1.5 cm) fabric around the whole template shape. Fold the seam allowances over the template and fasten the fabric onto it with basting stitches or by using a pink glue pen instead of sewing (Sewline). Make six hexagons from the same fabric and one from a different fabric. Place two hexagons on top of each other, right sides facing, and hand sew them carefully together using small stitches at the shape's edges. Make sure to fasten your thread at the beginning and end of each seam. Sew a complete flower. I find it easiest to start with the flower's center, and to sew the center's six contact sides around the flower circle. When these six seams are done, I remove the template at the center hexagon. It is easier to sew the side seams between the other hexagons when you can fold the hexagon flower. How you choose to sew the hexagons together may be a matter of taste. Make 15 flowers, and let the templates stay in all the hexagon petals around the flower's center.

Place a hexagon flower on top of a Four Patch block. Notice that the hexagon flower is not completely symmetrical. The hexagon's north/south sides are geometrically similar, and the east/west sides are the same, but the north and the west sides are not the same. It is, therefore, not arbitrary how you place the hexagon flower on the Four Patch block. The block's horizontal seam should correspond with two of the hexagon's seams. The block's vertical seam should pass beneath the upper and lower hexagons' middle.

Baste the hexagon flower onto the Four Patch block. I used my sewing machine with a straight stitch setting of 6 for basting. Use an invisible hand appliqué stitch, and fasten the hexagon flower to the block.

Cut away the block's fabric behind the hexagon flower, and make sure that you leave a seam allowance at the areas where you hand stitched. Remove all the hexagon templates and the basting stitches. Save the fabric pieces you have cut away from behind the hexagon flowers. You may want to use them for another project, since they can be the beginnings of a Four Patch block. All you have to do is to trim them.

ASSEMBLE THE PIECES

Trim the Four Patch block to the size you want. I used the lines on my large square ruler as guides. There are rulers that are made specifically for trimming large blocks, and it would be good to have one for this project. They have markings that show the center, and symmetrical control lines that go in all directions. You can also make your own plastic template with a drawing of the whole block. You can use it to make the cutting lines where you will be trimming. My cutting lines were 14½ x 14½ inches (37 cm x 37 cm).

FINISH IN STYLE

Sew all the blocks together, 3 blocks x 5 blocks, to make a quilt top. The borders have been cut 7½ inches (19 cm) wide for the sides, and 5½ inches (14 cm) wide for the quilt top's top and bottom. Place the quilt top on top of batting and backing, with the wrong sides towards the batting. Baste the layers together and quilt. Add binding strip.

A FINAL DIGRESSION

My daughter, Line Tolfsby Bakke, has sewn her own version of this quilt. She chose to make solid squares as background blocks for the hexagon flowers instead of my Four Patch blocks. Her fabric color choices are softer than mine. These attributes are reflected both in real life and in our quilts, mother/daughter different expressions. Notice the photo of her version of the quilt on the opposite page and a photo of mine hanging from a tree on page 100, and on the top right of this page.

CHAPTER 6

Trine's "Encyclopedia" of Tips & Tricks

This chapter begins with an overview of hand stitching and machine sewing. Even though, at the end, you have the same thing (a finished quilt!), the process of getting there is different with each method. I cover working without any special equipment, including hand stitching, how to make your own templates with added sewing lines (seam allowances), and machine sewing with ready-to-use patterns. I also provide information on appliqué, embroidery, and, finally, tips on assembling and finishing techniques.

Quilting without special equipment

Customers who come into our store, friends of mine, and readers of my books often ask: what is my favorite method of sewing? I always have a quick answer: stitching by hand. I love several things about that method of making and putting pieces together. I find it very relaxing for one thing, it is a portable activity (you can easily travel to a friend's house with a few blocks of fabric, a pair of scissors, and some thread), and it doesn't really need any special equipment. On the other hand, there are many lightweight sewing machines available these days, and they are meant for taking from place to place, like workshops, for example.

DESIGN AND STITCHING | **TRINE BAKKE**

Before you sew with either method, you will have to cut out your fabric. This first part is about the cutting. If you are using your sewing machine and a ready-made quilt pattern, you can skip to Step 9. If you plan to hand stitch, and design your own pattern (these two practices often go hand in hand), you'll need to make a template for cutting. You can buy ready-made templates for squares, triangles, rectangles, etc., made of heavy plastic (they can be found online or at a fabric or craft store) or stiff card stock (sometimes referred to as cardboard – but not the kind used to ship packages; that's corrugated cardboard and does not work well for pattern templates), or you can make them yourself out of the same materials. It's pretty likely that you'll have shapes around the house to use as a guide, and in the information below you'll learn how to make quilts without any special equipment.

1) GATHER YOUR FABRICS
Look around your home, at the flea market, and in fabric stores until you find material that you want to use. This part of the project may take awhile, so be patient. Collect material that you like, even if you do not know what you will want to sew. Look for fabrics that are similar in weight, weave, and quality. It is easiest to sew with fabrics that "give" and "build" in the same way. Bed linens, tablecloths, cotton dresses, and shirts are perfect for this purpose. Cut the garments apart so that you end up with flat pieces of fabrics. (I always save the fronts of shirts, too, with the button placket still attached. I use them as the backs of pillows.)

2) FIND SOMETHING THAT IS A SQUARE (OR A TRIANGLE, RECTANGLE, ETC.)
Look around your home or at the office for an easy-to-trace object. It could be a box, a tile left over after remodeling the bathroom, or a picture frame. This object should be easy to trace around and to hold in place while you're making it. As noted above, you'll be tracing this shape onto plastic or heavy card stock (like cereal or cracker boxes) to make a template, which you'll then use to draw on fabric for cutting. If you decide to use the plastic – a better option, because you can see through it and it can be used over and over again – an X-Acto knife or a box cutter helps a lot in the cutting, and a fine-line Sharpie pen works for tracing. I also recommend using a cutting board when cutting out the template material.

3) FIND A WORKSPACE
To accomplish Step 4, it is best if you have a solid surface to draw on; a coffee table or a dining room table are two good choices. A briefcase, a tray, or a computer pillow with a flat top may work well if you choose to sit on the sofa.

4) USE THE TEMPLATE TO CUT THE FABRIC
a) Choose a fabric, and cut a piece that is large enough for the shape you want to trace (including the ¼-inch [6 mm] seam allowance). By doing this, you are dealing with only one block; you do not have to plan out, for example, an entire quilt top as you draw.
b) Place the template on the wrong side of the fabric.
c) Draw around the shape with a pencil or sewing marker. You have now drawn a line that you will follow when you cut out the square. See Step 17 for drawing the sewing line (seam allowance).

5) USE A ROTARY CUTTER OR SCISSORS

If you do not already own a good pair of scissors, this is the time to consider purchasing one. Please know the life of your scissors will last much longer if you reserve them for cutting fabrics only. The same goes for the rotary cutter.

6) CUT

Cut out the fabric shape by carefully following the cutting line. Use a ruler if using a rotary cutter. Be precise and do not fudge.

7) CUT MANY PIECES

Just like the process of looking for and collecting fabric, cutting the pieces for your project will take time. Do a little now and then, when you're in the mood, and when you have some time. Be sure you have the seam allowance included when cutting. How many pieces you cut is dependent upon what kind of a project you are doing. Sometimes, I don't always have a clear plan when I begin, but I always start with the fabric I really like and cut to see how much I have, and then I move on to my next favorite. I don't necessarily keep track. Many times my plans don't become clear to me until after the pieces have been cut.

8) STITCH PIECES TOGETHER

Place two fabric pieces exactly on top of each other, right sides facing, and pin them together (see illustration at right).

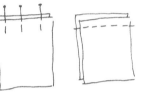

9) DECIDE IF YOU WILL USE A SEWING MACHINE OR STITCH BY HAND

The instructions below will give some tips on using a sewing machine for your project. If you decide to hand stitch your pieces together, go straight to Step 16.

10) CHOOSE A SEWING MACHINE AND THREAD

You will need a sewing machine that can sew a good, straight seam. To avoid any problems with it, be sure to read and follow the instructions that are provided for the machine. Additionally, stay away from inexpensive threads. I recommend Gütermann threads.

11) KEEP EVEN SEAM ALLOWANCES

I won't kid you; it can be a challenge to keep a completely even seam allowance when you are using a sewing machine. You have to concentrate on maintaining a very straight line, especially, at the beginning and the end of the seam. Check the Web for videos that may help and search for advice on "chain piecing by machine" and "pressing opposing seams."

12) SEW THE SEAMS

It is, by far, simplest to sew only straight seams; avoid those that are inset or angled. Begin by sewing two fabric pieces with right sides facing together. Then sew on another one, so that you have three pieces in a row. (See illustration top right, underneath photo.) Continue adding pieces, until you have four, five, or however many

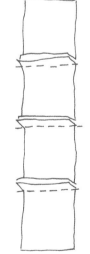

pieces you want to have in a row. Sew together another row of pieces, and set each row aside as you finish them. Sew as many rows as you need/want.

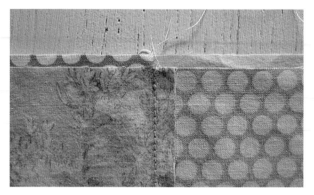

"meeting points"

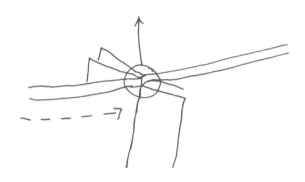

13) PRESS THE SEAM ALLOWANCES TOWARD ONE SIDE

Press every other row of fabric's seam allowances in a different direction. By doing this, you will be creating "meeting points." These points will help you make sharp seam-meeting points, where all four seams create a perfect cross. (See illustration above.)

14) SEW THE ROWS TOGETHER TO MAKE A QUILT TOP

Choose two sewn rows, and place them on top of each other, right sides facing; make sure the seam allowances are pressed in different directions. Once the two rows are placed evenly on top of the other, pin in place, and sew the whole length of the rows together. Press the new seam allowance. Continue to sew one row of fabric pieces next to the previous, until your quilt top is the size you want it to be. (See illustration at right.)

15) HAND STITCHING

Here are my tips and instructions for hand stitching.

16) FIND A SMALL RULER

You will need a ruler that you will use to draw the sewing lines on your piece of fabric. When your piece of fabric has been marked appropriately, it should have a drawing of a square placed a little distance from the fabric's edges. It is best to use a ruler that is between ¼ and 1 inch (0.6 and 2.5 cm) wide. It should be at least as long as your fabric square. From my experience, you may find just such a ruler in your junk drawer, in the tool chest, or in a school backpack. Once in need, I used a nail file.

17) ADD THE SEAM ALLOWANCE

Draw the width of the ¼-inch (6 mm) ruler on all sides of the square. Place the ruler accurately along one of the square's drawn edges. Draw, with a pencil, along the ruler's outer edge.

Repeat the process around the entire square. You have now drawn the cutting line, which includes the ¼-inch (6 mm) seam allowance. (See illustration.)

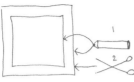

18) BRING OUT THE HAND-STITCHING TOOLS

Needle: You can use any needle, but the best is to use a good-quality, thin needle with the smallest eye that you can find. The needle will then glide through the fabrics with as little resistance as possible. If you are going to sew many seams over a longer period of time, you should be thinking about the quality of the needle when you are looking for one. If you are only interested in trying the hand-stitching method, any needle will do – you can find them in the sewing kits that nicer hotels provide, or at grocery stores.

Thread: Use a neutral color thread. I sew a lot of my projects using a beige-colored polyester thread. If you do not have this kind of thread on hand, use what you have.

Scissors: Use the same scissors you used for cutting the fabric. Or you may prefer a pair of small embroidery scissors, or thread cutters.

Pins: Pins are helpful. Stay away from heads that are plastic – not good when pressing, because the heat could melt the plastic!

19) HAND STITCH TWO PIECES OF FABRIC TOGETHER

a) Place two pieces of fabric exactly on top of each other, right sides facing. Pin them together by placing the pins at a right angle to the seam you are going to stitch.

b) Begin with your needle and a knot in the thread at the start of the stitching line.

c) Sew! Use regular running stitches for the seam.

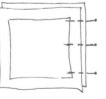

d) Follow the drawn stitching lines on one side of the fabric piece when you sew. You may want to make a backstitch now and then to reinforce your seam. A backstitch is to sew on top of the same spot two times. You are only going to sew to the end of the stitching line and not to the end of the fabric piece. Turn your piece over, and check if your seam is somewhat in place on the other piece's stitching line.

e) At the end of the stitching line, knot your thread again, and remove the pins.

20) PRESS THE SEAM

Open up the two pieces of fabric, and make sure that they have been stitched together well. Use an iron or your fingers to press the seam allowances apart. Do not pull or push on the pieces.

21) CONTINUE SEWING UNTIL YOU HAVE A ROW OF FABRIC PIECES

Sew an appropriately long row of square fabric pieces together. Some people like to sew two sets of two together, then sew four and four pieces, and so forth. Others just add one piece to the next piece until their row of square fabric pieces is long enough. Sew a number of rows.

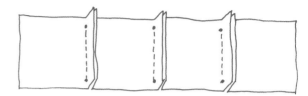

22) SEW THE ROWS TOGETHER

Place two rows of fabric pieces on top of each other, right sides facing, and edges lining up. Pin. Make sure that all corners meet exactly at the other corners. Hand stitch as you usually do. Make sure that you do not sew to the end of the fabric piece, but only the length of the stitching line on each square. Again, you can choose if you want to sew two sets of two rows together, or four sets of four rows, and so on. Or you may choose to sew one row after the other, adding one at a time. Press seam allowances as you sew.

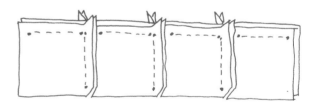

Quilting with a pattern

WHY FOLLOW A PATTERN?

So far, I have given tips and instructions on hand stitching and creating your own pattern templates. However, there are many reasons to follow someone else's pattern instead. First, because it's easier! If you're new to quilting, using a ready-made pattern with step-by-step instructions may be the best first step. Maybe you like the proportions of a pattern? Maybe you want your finished work to be of a certain size? Maybe you find it pleasurable that someone else has thought through all the dimensions and seam allowances that will work well together? I am sure that there are many more good reasons for using a pattern.

In the explanations for hand stitching and machine sewing given on the previous pages, you were advised to find something around the house to draw your shape around. Now, you will trace a pattern from this book with its already determined dimensions, onto your choice of template material.

MAKING A TEMPLATE

It is easiest to use a template made of plastic. A plastic template can be used over and over, and it's helpful that you can see through it when tracing. Sheets of the plastic are readily available in fabric or hobby/craft stores. Place the plastic on top of a pattern (only if you have a full-sized pattern; if you have to enlarge, do that first before making the cutting template) and trace, using a Sharpie pen, the design onto the plastic. The plastic should be as thick as possible. Make sure that your drawing is permanent and does not smudge.

Cut out your templates with a "frame" for the projects that you will be stitching by hand (see the illustration on page 109, Step 17). The frame's outer lines are the cutting lines, and the inner lines are the stitching lines. The thicker your plastic template is, the easier it will be to trace its outline without the template's shape distorting. You can also make two templates for the same shape, one for the cutting lines and one for the stitching lines. An alternative is to make one template with only the cutting lines, and as a sewing aid, you can make little holes in the template: Make a small hole in the plastic template at all the corners where seams meet. Use a sharp tapestry needle, and heat it over a candle flame before you push it through the plastic where you want holes. Now you have a template ready for use.

For machine sewing, you only make one template with the cutting lines. Use the template(s) as described on page 107, Step 4. Add a seam allowance around all the template's sides, if it has not already been included in the shape.

You can also use cardboard for your templates if you do not have any plastic. Look through your paper recycling bin, and see if you can find some usable cardboard, such as a cereal or cracker box, or the board from the back of a legal pad for making templates. The simplest method to transfer the drawn template onto the cardboard is to use vellum, parchment, or tracing paper. Draw the image that you can see through your paper onto the tracing paper, and with spray or a glue pen, attach the tracing paper onto the cardboard. Cut out the image, and your the template is ready for use. You can also make a copy of the image on a photocopy machine by spray gluing the copy to the cardboard, and then cutting out the template.

HAND STITCHING OVER PAPER

You may be familiar with English paper piecing (look online for detailed instructions). By using this technique, you'll find greater precision in your quilt blocks or full quilt. Briefly, the fabric pieces in a block each get wrapped around a shaped paper piece (typically made of plain copy paper if you aren't using ready-made templates) and are then basted with a contrasting thread and long running stitch to the wrong side of the fabric. Note: It may be wise, in some cases, to make an extended seam allowance beyond the usual ¼ inch (6 mm).

When you're ready to attach pieces, place right sides together and join them with a small whipstitch that catches only the edge of the fabric. As you continue to build and piece your blocks, you will have to pull out the basting stitches. I recommend using ready-to-use templates that you can buy. If you do not have a store close to you that sell these templates, you can buy them online.

BUSINESS AND MAGAZINE CARDS

Using old or obsolete business cards or the cards that are inserted into magazines are an alternative to buying ready-made templates. Use the same instructions as on the previous page ("Hand

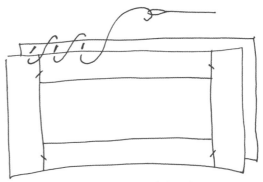

Joining two pieces with shaped blocks with whip stitches at the fabric's edge

Stitching Over Paper"), although it is best to cut and wrap each pattern shape before you begin to join the fabric into a block. See the illustration on the right. Trace and cut your shapes, pin or paper-clip a business card to the wrong side of the fabric, and cut it out with a seam allowance on each side. Try to cut wide seam allowances evenly and equally.

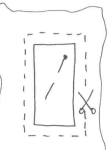

QUILTING WITH SPECIAL EQUIPMENT

There is a huge selection of specialty tools available that will make quilting both fun and "easy." I recommend everything! Sign up for a workshop, check out what is available online, ask what is available at any sewing or crafting supplies store, visit quilting shows, become a member of a quilting group, and learn! I have been sewing for more than 25 years, and I have yet to master everything there is to learn.

Embroidery

There are so many different embroidery stitches. I prefer the simple ones. The same stitches that you used to sew pieces together are also wonderful embroidery stitches. Choose a thicker, nicer thread when you are embroidering.

Backstitches are also gratifying to use. See illustration below.

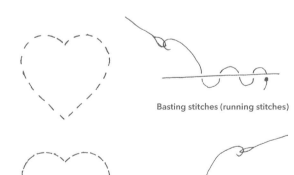

Basting stitches (running stitches)

Backstitches

TOOLS

A needle, thread, and fabric – that is all that you need. If you choose a beautiful fabric and a nice embroidery thread, your work is halfway there. The fabric you choose may be a piece of linen, a checkered kitchen towel, or a piece of a wool blanket.

Some people prefer to embroider with an embroidery hoop. Others choose to reinforce their fabric with a very thin piece of flannel that resembles batting. The reason they do this is to give the embroidery more heft. However, you will manage quite well without any of these tools. The only thing to watch out for is that you do not pull the embroidery thread so tightly that the fabric bunches up.

TRANSFER PATTERNS

Embroideries done without any patterns are sure winners. You may want to follow the checkerboard pattern on a kitchen towel, or just doodle with embroidery thread in different colors. You could study a design that you like, and then embroider your own stylized version of the design. There are many designs that can be broken down into geometric shapes like squares, half circles, and lines.

If you are the kind of person who likes more structure, you can transfer a line pattern onto your piece of fabric. You will then follow this line drawing as you embroider. There are several ways of transferring the pattern onto a piece of fabric.

a) Select a window where sunlight is shining through toward you. Fasten, with tape, the original design onto the window, and then tape a piece of fabric over the design. You will now be able to see the original line drawing through the fabric. Of course, your fabric has to be of a light color and not too tightly woven. Denim fabrics will not work with this method. Make continuous dots with a pencil on the fabric you will embroider, and begin to sew.

b) Another option is to trace the pattern onto a tracing or vellum paper with a soft pencil. Place the tracing paper on the embroidery fabric with the pencil drawing down on the fabric. Draw the pattern again, now on the tracing paper's back side, following the image you can see through the paper. The first pencil drawing will transfer onto the fabric, and you will have a pattern to follow when you start to embroider.

c) Draw the image with an alcohol ink marker onto a piece of tulle. Let the marker ink dry completely. Place the tulle on top of an embroidery fabric, and use a pencil to trace the design by making dots through the tulle's holes.

d) You may want to buy some transfer aids from a crafting supplies store. Among many options, there are markers with disappearing ink, and transfer paper that can be run through a copier.

SHOULD THE BACK BE AS BEAUTIFUL AS THE FRONT?

No, that is not necessary. Concentrate instead on the joy you find in doing embroideries. If you are worried about comments, make sure to finish your embroidery in such a way that no one can turn it around to look at the back side. Mounting your embroidery tightly inside a picture frame could just be the solution. You could also sew your artwork onto another piece of fabric that afterward is sewn onto a pillowcase.

WILL THE PENCIL LINE DISAPPEAR DURING LAUNDERING?

The pencil line will not always disappear. To be on the safe side, I recommend a light hand on the pencil when you are transferring your pattern. Backstitches will cover most of the drawn lines, so this type of a stitch is best to use if you are worried about the pencil line remaining on the fabric after it has been laundered. A good rule to go by is to draw the lines as if the pencil lines will never be removed. The wish to see the pattern while you are embroidering is often in conflict with the desire to have all the guidelines gone by the time you are done!

Appliqués

Cut out a shape, for example, a heart in a fabric with a flower pattern. Sew the heart onto a piece of denim, and suddenly you have done an appliqué. That is how easy it is.

TOOLS

All you will need is a needle, some thread, a pair of scissors, and some fabric. You can enjoy transferring a pattern onto a piece of paper, and then fastening this pattern paper onto a piece of fabric before you cut out the shape. Use some of the same techniques that have been described for embroidery when you want to make templates for appliqués.

Overcast Stitch

APPLIQUÉ STITCHES

Choose your appliqué stitches based upon how much you will launder the finished product. Many of my appliqué projects are framed under glass; those projects will not be laundered, ever. I often use an overcast stitch for my appliques. it is quick to use quick to sew, and in my opinion, very decorative. The thread you use will add charm. If you choose an unexpected color of thread, you may be surprised by how unique your appliqué is!

Blanket Stitch

Alternatively, you can use blanket stitches if you do not like that the appliqué fabric's raw edges become untidy after being laundered. I do not mind if the edges are messy, so I seldom take the time to sew blanket stitches. However, many people find peace of mind sewing blanket stitches while watching TV.

START IN THE BACK AND WORK FORWARD

When you are making an appliqué that consists of several overlapping pieces, you must think about the layering sequences. Let us say that you are making a wreath with stems, leaves, and flowers. You must build up this appliqué in such a way that one piece covers another and the most important parts are placed on the top.

THE FIRST SPECIALTY TOOL!

If you are going to shop for only one tool, the time has come for a double-sided fusible webbing that adheres to a fabric with the aid of heat from an iron. The adhesive is protected by paper on at least one of the sides, or possibly both, depending upon the manufacturer. Be sure to follow the manufacturer's instructions carefully when you use a webbing. By not following the manufacturer's instructions, the process of using a fusible webbing becomes unnecessarily complex and imprecise, and you can get adhesive on your iron, which will create a mess.

1. Draw the shape (heart) on the webbing's paper side. It does not matter which side you choose if your webbing has paper on both sides.

Double-sided fusible webbing

2. Cut well outside the heart shape so that you get more of the webbing along with the drawn heart.

3. Remove the paper on the side that you have not drawn.

4. Place the webbing with the heart up, on top of the fabric's wrong side.

The heart fabric's wrong side

5. Press with an iron on a medium heat setting for a few seconds.

6. Let it cool.

7. Carefully cut out the heart following the drawn lines.

8. Pull off the paper.

9. Place the fabric heart, with the right side up, on top of the appliqué fabric, also with the right side up.

Another fabric's right side

10. Press the heart with an iron on a medium heat setting for a few seconds.

11. Let it cool.

The heart has now been securely attached to the background fabric, but it will not stay in place during laundering unless you sew it, regardless of what the ads say.

If your appliqué is a picture that you want to frame under glass, then sewing may not be strictly necessary to keep your image in place. However, the stitches add a lot to the image on an aesthetic level, so you may want to draw them in or embroider them.

It will be important to stitch all around your appliqué, if it is going to be on something that will be worn a lot and often laundered.

Finishing

A beautiful piece of handwork, whether it's a pillow cover, table runner, or quilt top, can provide an immense amount of pleasure. Why not finish it in a style that complements your work? This section provides information and tips for several finishing possibilities. Choose the method that suits your expertise and your wallet. FYI: It is possible to buy yourself out of a tough spot by letting professionals do the quilting!

SEW A PILLOW

A pillow provides a great opportunity to try out many kinds of finishing. It's easy to handle (small), and you can complete the entire project in a matter of hours. I will use it here as an example of the possibilities of tidying everything up.

If your pillow front includes a wonderful patchwork, embroidery, or appliqué, make sure it is ready (pressed, loose threads cut, seam allowances trimmed, etc.) for the final finishing steps. Cut out a piece of fabric for the back of the pillow that's the same size as the front. Place the two pieces on top of each other, right sides facing. Sew almost around the entire pillow cover, but leave an opening in the bottom seam. Turn the pillow cover inside out through this opening, press, and insert a pillow insert through the same opening. Hand stitch the opening shut, and you are done!

PILLOW TRICKS

You can make the pillow even nicer by trying some of these techniques. Here are a few tips:

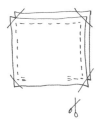

- Trim the seam allowances at the corners, it will make your pillow look better.

- Adjust the size of your decorative front so that it fits with readily-available pillow inserts, or inserts that you already own. I have learned that the sewn pillow cover looks best if you make the pillow's front fabric of the same size as the pillow insert. Do not add any extra seam allowances. So, a good starting point is to get the pillow insert first.

- Try overlapping some pieces of fabric on the back of the pillow for added texture.

- Make a pillow back from a shirt front. Trim it and use the button placket as the opening. If there is not enough fabric for the pillow back from your shirt, just add on other fabrics until the piece is large enough. Plan and cut the pillow cover's back pieces in such a way that you avoid sewing into buttons.

- Instead of using a shirt front with button placket on the back, try it on the front!

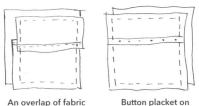

| An overlap of fabric | Button placket on the pillow front |

Finish your runner by sewing all around the edges on the wrong side and turning it inside out. Trim the seam allowances at the corners.

Sew the opening shut. Sew a seam around all the outer edges on the right side. Fasten the layers together with ← buttons, sewn stitches, or yarn knots.

TABLE RUNNER

Follow the instructions for "Sew a Pillow" on the previous page, but after you trim the seam allowances at the corners, turn the project inside out, and press, you will sew the opening shut. Fasten the two layers together with a few stitches at some chosen locations, so that the two layers act as one; wool can sometimes "slide" around, so I often sew on buttons through both layers to keep that from happening. You may choose to make wool yarn knots through the layers. Some people prefer to sew a seam all around the outer edges on the outside to stabilize the layers additionally.

PLATE CORNERS

Let us say that you have sewn your layers together on the wrong side, as described above, and that you are not completely satisfied with the corners. It can be difficult to make them all sharp and even. The solution is to round the corners. Try this little trick: Place the quilt top and backing on top of each other, right sides facing. Sew a seam almost around all the edges. Leave an opening where you can turn the project inside out, but before you do this, get a plate. Place the plate, with the bottom up, at one of the corners. Align the plate's edges with the sewn seams. Place one piece of tape exactly at each of the points where the edge of the plate and a seam meet. Use the plate to draw a bow between the two seams. Move the plate to the next corner, use the pieces of tape to place the plate in the same position as before, and draw another bow. Repeat the process at the other two corners. Next, sew a seam following the drawn rounded lines, trim the seam allowances, and cut perpendicular nicks into the seam allowances at the bows. Turn it inside out, press, and sew the opening shut.

HOW TO BUTCHER A BLAZER

A wool blazer is a little gold mine for anyone who sews; its various parts can be used on many different projects. Before you begin cutting it apart, wash the blazer on a wool temperature setting, and dry flat. Always wash the items that you have made from the blazer's parts on the same temperature setting.

- Use the blazer's front with the buttons for something that you want to open and close, for example, the back of pillow covers.

- Use the pockets from the blazer as inside pockets on a tote bag.

- Use the sleeves as storage for plastic bags or the beginnings of a purse.

- Sew a zigzag seam over all raw edges to make sure that all the loose threads do not get tangled during multiple launderings.

- Sew slowly and use a strong needle, for example, a needle for denim fabric.

- Sew rounded corners on the pillow or trim the seam allowances at the corners if you prefer sharp corners.

- Cut up the blazer into pieces; you can trim the pieces, as needed, later. Try to remove interlinings, double layers, and other tailoring pieces, if you want flat pieces of fabric.

TUBE AND BIAS TAPE

This is another way to finish your quilt or runner. Sew together your project's front and back sides to make a cylinder or a tube. Lay the tube flat on a surface, and press. Sew a seam on the tube's outside edges along the two sides that have been sewn together. Finish off the two raw sides with bias tapes. Keep the layers together with sewn buttons or yarn knots as described earlier.

Bias tape at tube finishing

Splice the bias tape

BIAS TAPE OR BINDING STRIP?

You can buy bias tape by the yard, and it can be used to edge your sewn projects. A bias tape is a is a folded "ribbon" of fabric that covers the quilt's raw edges – it can also add a fun color accent to your project. When I mention bias tape, I mean a piece that is 2½ inches wide. Bias tapes have been cut diagonally across the fabric's grain. This is necessary to make the tapes flexible, and to give them the ability to "mold" into different shapes.

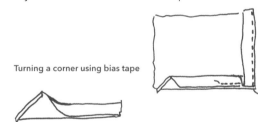

Turning a corner using bias tape

PIECING BIAS TAPES

You do not have to use bias tapes if you are making projects without rounded edges. Bias tapes also work on straight runs, but they are technically not necessary. You may as well make your own binding strips for these areas.

Instructions for making binding strips: Cut a long strip of fabric, for example 2½" (6.4 cm) wide. Fold the fabric strip in two along the length, and iron it along the fold. Your strip will now be 1¼" (3.18 cm) wide. Make sure that the fabric's right side is on the strip's outside. Place the fabric strip's raw edge along a quilt's raw edge. Sew the strip in place, fold the strip over on to the quilt's back side, and sew the binding strip, with a hem, on to the backing.

Sew on bias tape or a binding strip at all of the quilt's edges. The easiest way to do this is to cut the bias tape or binding strip into four different pieces, and attach each piece, one at a time, at each of the quilt's edges. You must fold under and sew the tape or the binding strip nicely at the corners. Be sure to add a little extra length to the last bias tape or binding strip, so that you have enough material to overlap the first piece of bias tape/binding strip and fold the end under.

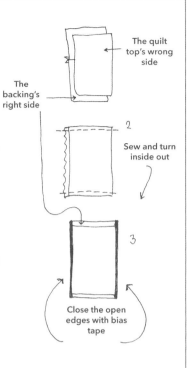

The quilt top's wrong side

The backing's right side

2

Sew and turn inside out

3

Close the open edges with bias tape

It is more complicated to sew one length of bias tape or binding strip around an entire quilt in one operation. Study the drawing, and foremost, ask someone who has experience in doing this to show you how it is done. I have written about the mistakes that people make when they use fusible webbing (see "Appliqués" on page 112). Making mistakes while adding a bias tape or a binding strip while finishing off a quilt are the next most common mistakes that sewers made. Among the mistakes that I have often seen are diagonal corners that are not diagonal. Choose some of my other finishing suggestions if you are happy to live without these challenges in your everyday life!

BATTING OR NOT?

If you want to give your quilt heft, loft, texture, and "wrinkle-shrinkage," add a batting sandwiched inside your quilt. I have omitted the whole batting discussion on purpose, because adding batting to your projects is not an absolute necessity. However, if you want to add batting, you must know that the selections available are enormous, and that there is not one answer to the question of which batting is the right one – although, I do have my favorites and have mentioned them on some projects.

Let us say that you are not going to buy batting at one of the specialty stores, but would rather find something you can use at home or at a flea market: Flannel sheets that have been washed innumerable times and old wool blankets are good choices. Make sure that you launder this kind of "batting" before you use it. Wool must always be washed on the same temperature setting that you will use to launder the finished quilt. The quilt's sandwiched layers must be held together in place in some fashion. The batting must, at least, be fastened along the quilt's outer edges.

Are you going to buy some batting? You should know that a batting's price and quality are closely related. Make sure to check if the batting that you are going to buy "drapes" the way you want it to. A major rule is that batting bought from quality stores should never be washed before use. I am not sure that the same goes for batting bought from discount stores. You must make sure that the batting that you buy can take laundering when it has been sandwiched inside your quilt. My experience is that cotton batting must be quilted, if you want to launder it to avoid shrinkage or shrinkage that distorts the quilt's shape. Synthetic batting behaves differently, and can be used without being quilted.

I prefer to use only cotton batting in different thicknesses for my projects. Regardless of the type of projects, be it makeup bags, runners, quilts, purses, or other things, I always sew the batting in place.

When making quilts, it is important to make sure that the batting fibers do not migrate (work their way through the fabrics) during laundering. The types of batting that are labeled needle-punched or "made for quilting" should be a safe selection. The less expensive batting's fibers cannot be guaranteed not to migrate.

I will repeat that there is not one type of batting that is the right one. It all comes down to your taste, what you envision when you think about how your project will feel to hold, how it feels around your body, and how it drapes. You can find synthetic batting, and batting that is made from silk, wool, bamboo, and cotton. Many of these different types of batting come in different thicknesses, with or without adhesives, with or without shrinkage, for sale by the yard or as sheets, inexpensive, and expensive. It is a jungle out there, and my best advice is to find your way by experimenting with the different types of batting. Or you may simply choose to do as I have done, and use only cotton batting from Quilters Dream, flannel sheets, and old wool blankets.

KNOTS OR STITCHES?

Regardless of whether you use batting or not, the quilts' and runners' front sides must somehow be held in place along with their back sides. The easiest way to accomplish this is to sew on buttons through both layers, evenly distributed throughout one of the surfaces, and consequently keep both sides, with or without batting, in place. You can also sew a few stitches "in place," evenly distributed, and in this manner fasten the layers together. Sewn knots can be decorative as well.

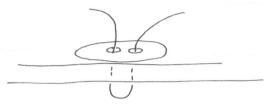

The time-honored method of keeping the layers together, is, of course, quilting. You can sew seams by hand using a running stitch or on a sewing machine and they will hold all the layers in place. Your stitches can be sewn following many different, fancy patterns, yet sewing rows of parallel seams is a beautiful quilting pattern. Quilting is a vast field, and you can seek out knowledge online, and look at instructional videos. I recommend attending some quilting workshops. There is also always the option of letting professional quilters do the work for you. I have done that for several of the quilts in this book.

Embroidered Wool Quilt, see page 70

PATTERNS

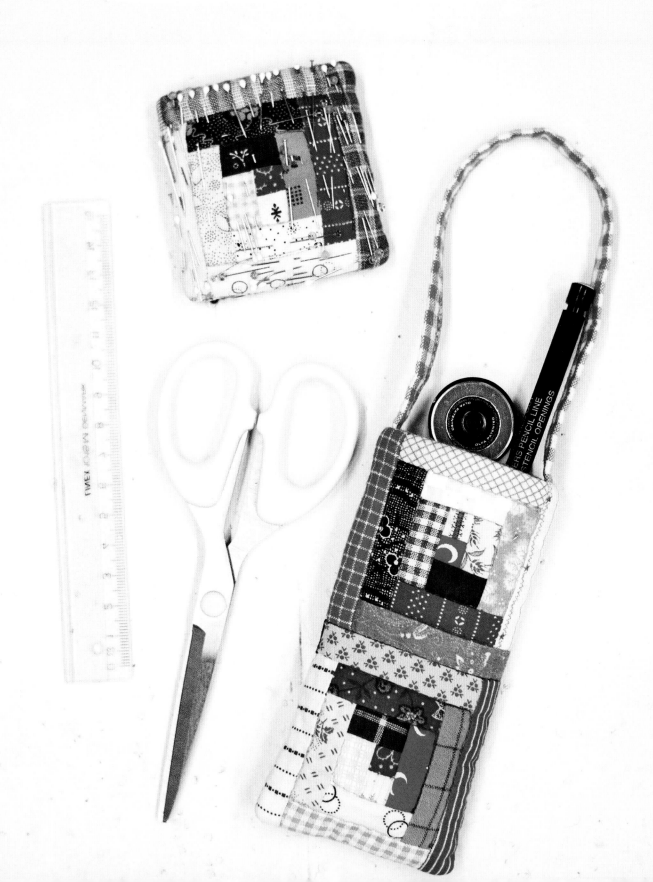

Starry Night Quilt with Appliquéd Bolster , page 72

100% of actual size

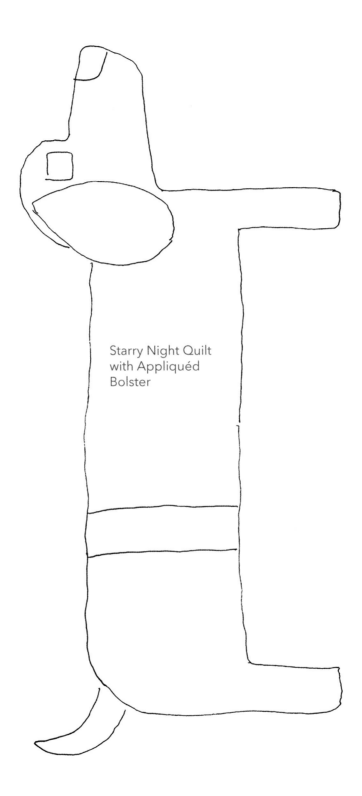

Starry Night Quilt
with Appliquéd
Bolster

Christmas Stocking, page 18

45% of actual size;
enlarge by 155%

Christmas Stocking

"Four Patch" Wool Bolster, page 16

100% of actual size

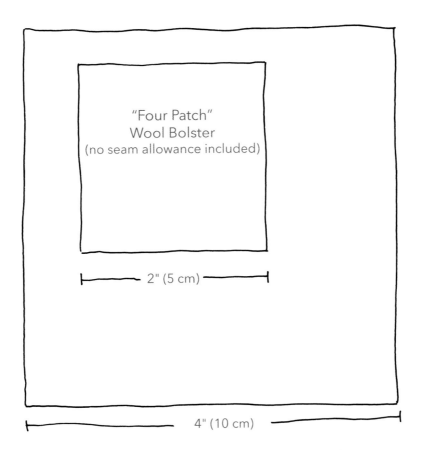

"Four Patch"
Wool Bolster
(no seam allowance included)

2" (5 cm)

4" (10 cm)

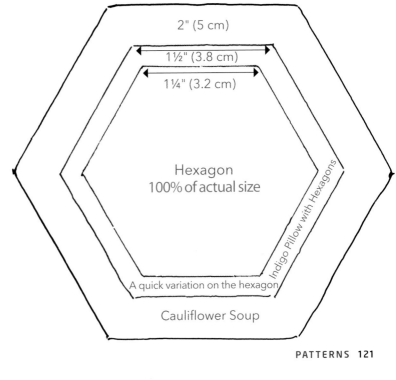

2" (5 cm)

1½" (3.8 cm)

1¼" (3.2 cm)

Hexagon
100% of actual size

Indigo Pillow with Hexagons

A quick variation on the hexagon

Cauliflower Soup

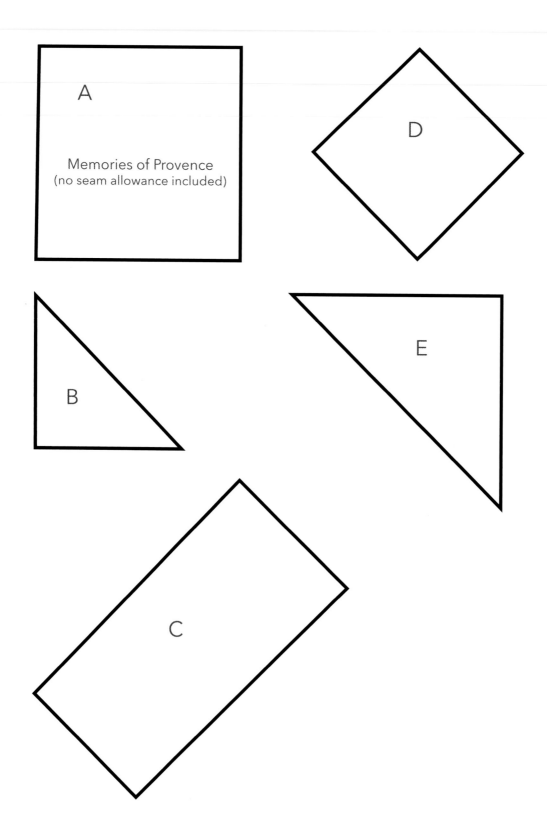

A

Memories of Provence
(no seam allowance included)

D

B

E

C

Clamshell, page 90

100% of actual size

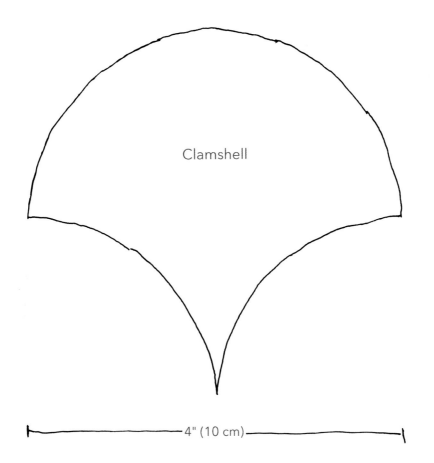

Clamshell

4" (10 cm)

Choo-choo Baby Blanket, page 34

100% of actual size

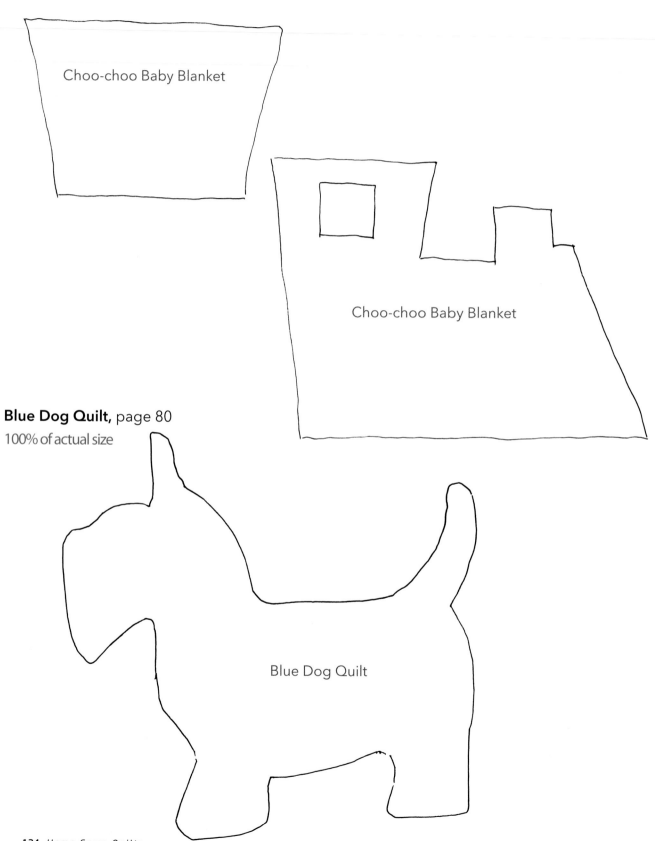

Choo-choo Baby Blanket

Choo-choo Baby Blanket

Blue Dog Quilt, page 80

100% of actual size

Blue Dog Quilt

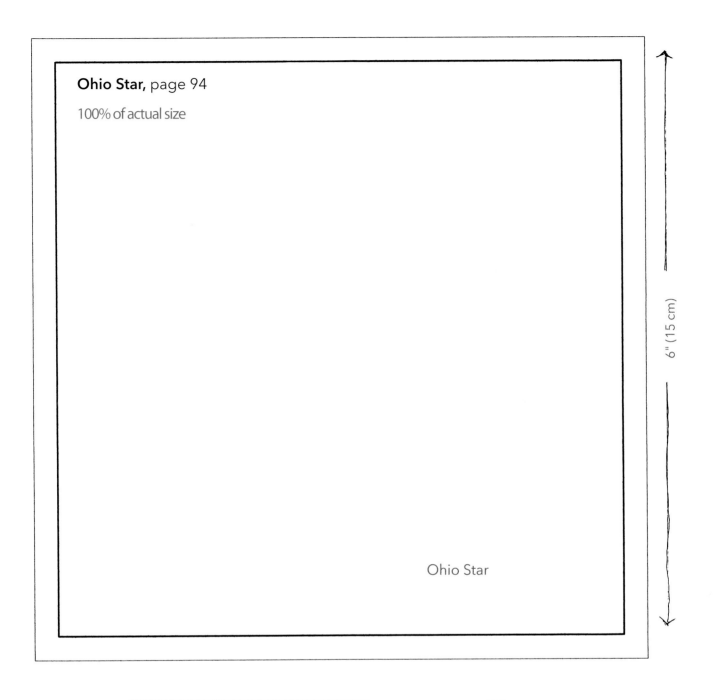

Ohio Star, page 94

100% of actual size

Ohio Star

6" (15 cm)

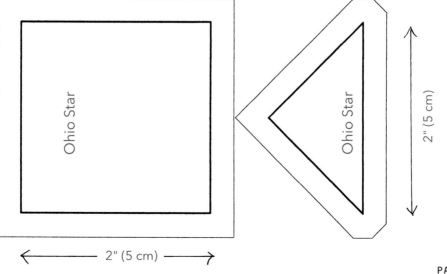

Ohio Star

Ohio Star

2" (5 cm)

2" (5 cm)

Wool Bag with a Ten-point Star Appliqué, page 40

60% of actual size;
enlarge by 140%

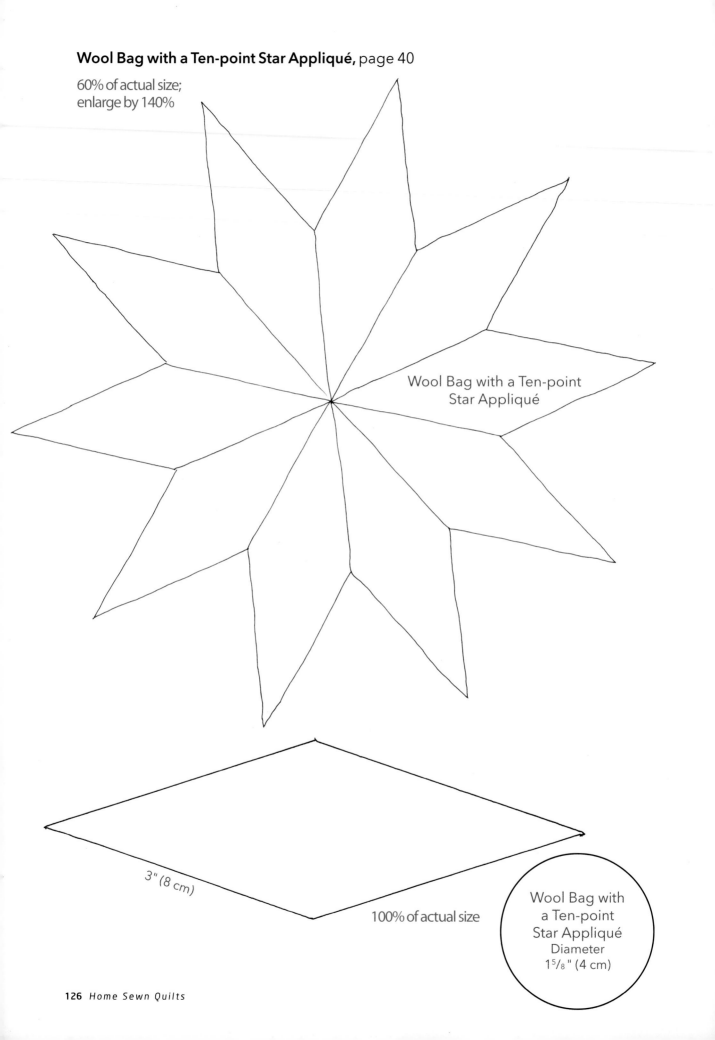

Wool Bag with a Ten-point
Star Appliqué

3" (8 cm)

100% of actual size

Wool Bag with
a Ten-point
Star Appliqué
Diameter
1⅝" (4 cm)

Linen and Wool Bag with Dresden Appliqué, page 38

60% of actual size;
enlarge by 140%

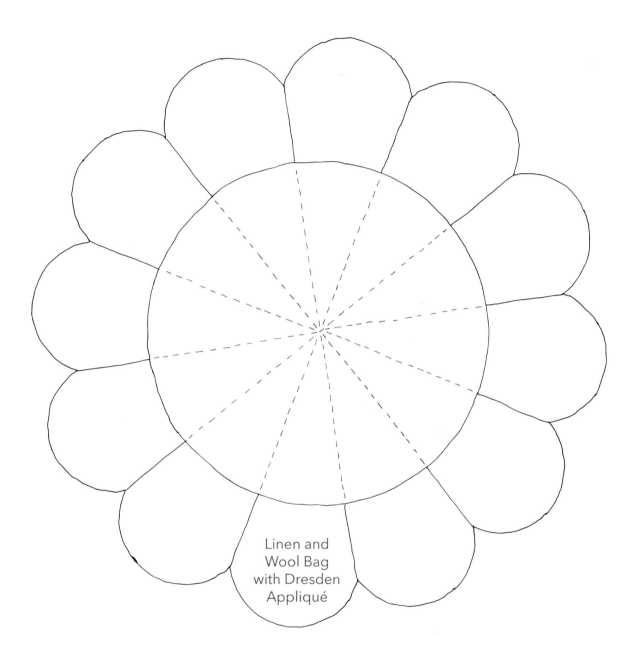

Linen and
Wool Bag
with Dresden
Appliqué

Acknowledgments

A big thank-you to all of the supporters and friends of Lappe Markeriet – our quilting and fabric shop wouldn't be the same without you. As well, thanks to our good neighbors in Bærums Verk., especially Ulla and her husband, Bob Laycock who generously allowed us to take many of the photographs in this book at their beautiful hotel and restaurant, Værtshuset.

This book is dedicated to our youngest son, Mikkel Bakke. He is the smartest thing we have done.

-Trine Bakke

Sellers Publishing wishes to thank author Trine Bakke for her outstanding work on this book. Our appreciation also goes to the Norwegian publisher, Cappelen Damm; as always, they are a joy to work with.

We couldn't have created this book without the help of translator Margaret Berge Hartge; a huge thank-you to her – she always exceeds expectations. Copyeditor Alissa Cyphers was an integral part of the team; her talent and contributions were so very welcome, along with Charlotte Cromwell, production editor, and managing editor, Mary Baldwin, who kept it all together.

-Robin Haywood